Copier Creations

Also by Paul Fleischman

Picture Books
Time Train
Shadow Play
Rondo in C
The Birthday Tree

Novels
Bull Run
Townsend's Warbler
The Borning Room
Saturnalia
Rear-View Mirrors
Path of the Pale Horse
The Half-A-Moon Inn

Short Story Collections
Coming-and-Going Men: Four Tales
Graven Images: Three Stories

Poetry
Joyful Noise: Poems for Two Voices
I Am Phoenix: Poems for Two Voices

Copier Creations

Using Copy Machines to Make Decals, Silhouettes, Flip Books, Films, and Much More!

By Paul Fleischman • Illustrated by David Cain

HarperCollins*Publishers*

For Lance, Kathy, Annelise,

and Noël Chilton—who are irreproducible

—P.F.

Copier Creations

Using Copy Machines to Make Decals, Silhouettes, Flip Books, Films, and Much More!

Text copyright © 1993 by Paul Fleischman

Illustrations copyright © 1993 by David Cain

Printed in the United States of America. For information address HarperCollins Children's Books, a division of HarperCollins Publishers, 10 East 53rd Street, New York, NY 10022.

1 2 3 4 5 6 7 8 9 10

First Edition

Library of Congress Cataloging-in-Publication Data

Fleischman, Paul

   Copier creations ; using copy machines to make decals, silhouettes, flip books, films, and much more! / by Paul Fleischman ; illustrated by David Cain.

     p.   cm.

   Includes bibliographical references.

   Summary: A creative guide to using copy machines to produce silhouettes, miniatures, decals, flip books, and other kinds of inexpensive artwork.

   ISBN 0-06-021052-4. — ISBN 0-06-021053-2 (lib. bdg.)

   1. Copy art—Juvenile literature. [1. Copy art.] I. Cain, David, ill. II. Title.

NE3000.F59 1993   91-45413

760—dc20   CIP

                                                                                      AC

Contents

Introduction

Were Rembrandt alive today, he'd likely be producing masterpieces on the copy machine. If Leonardo da Vinci were living, he'd no doubt have built his own. Copiers are wondrous artistic tools. They produce striking creations, yet are simple to use. They're clean. They're inexpensive. They're readily available. Your final product appears in an instant, needn't

dry, and can itself be copied. Best of all, with the use of clip art, copiers allow children (and adults) who find drawing difficult to produce professional-looking artwork. They can be used to make stationery, silhouettes, puzzles, decals for car windows, badges for clothing, flip books, even films.

The projects in this book are intended for readers old enough to read a ruler, handle a cutting knife, and go to the library and copy shop on their own. Younger artists can take part with a little adult assistance. The projects get more complex—and the results more exciting—as you proceed through the book.

Most people use copiers only to copy. Here you'll learn to use them to combine, alter, construct, and create.

Copiers and Where to Find Them

Most public libraries have copy machines. They can be found as well in some post offices and drugstores. Many of these machines don't produce sharp copies and don't allow you to reduce or enlarge what you're copying. Perhaps you can use a copier at one of your parents' workplaces. Most likely, though, you'll want to go to a copy shop. These will probably be listed in the phone book under "Copying," "Duplicating," or "Photo-copying."

Copy shops offer nearly everything you'll need. Most have self-service machines, where you can make your original bigger or smaller or lighter or darker without having to tell anyone what you want done. These machines are less expensive to use than those in libraries and other public places and usually make better copies. They'll probably offer more paper sizes as well.

Behind the counter, the clerks can make copies on colored paper, heavier papers, and clear plastic trans-parencies. Many shops can make single-color or full-color copies, extra-large copies, and iron-on transfers. Binding, stapling, and paper cutting are also commonly available. Find out the cost of these services first.

Try to pick a shop that has more than one self-service machine, as well as work space for cutting and gluing. If you need the behind-the-counter services, don't hesitate to tell the clerk exactly what you want. Keep in mind that you may have to wait awhile before a clerk gets to your job. It's best to be there when your job is run, so that you can be shown a proof (a test copy) to check. If possible, choose a time when the shop isn't thronged.

Supplies

With the tools and materials below, you'll be able to make all the projects in this book. Most copy shops sell some of these supplies or have them available at no charge. The others can be bought at a stationery store. Consider putting a kit together that you can take to the copy shop. This will save on trips back and forth.

Paper

Copy machines use copy paper, which is designed to be copied onto. You'll glue artwork and words onto copy paper also. The three most common sizes are 8½" x 11" (standard), 8½" x 14" (legal size), and 11" x 17". Some copy shops offer larger sizes as well. All will sell you blank sheets to work on. You can buy a ream (500 sheets) of copy paper at a stationery store. Most copy shops have many colors available as well as many weights of paper. Card stock, the heaviest, is used in many of the projects in this book.

Pens

You'll need black felt-tip pens, both fine and broad point. For full-color copies, use colored highlighting pens. For making guidelines that you don't want the copier to print, use a fine-point yellow felt pen.

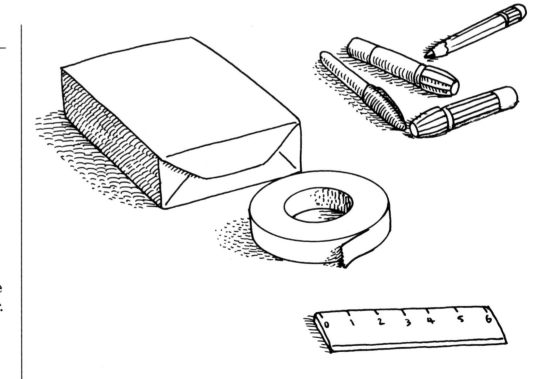

Whiteout

This is the copy artist's eraser. There are three different kinds: for covering up things written or drawn in ink, typed on a typewriter, or produced on a copy machine. You'll need all three.

A Folder

Get the kind with pockets inside. This will protect the artwork you take to the copy shop and the copies you bring home.

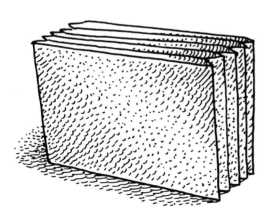

Correction Tape

This tape is white, won't show up on copies, and comes in several widths. It's much easier to use than whiteout when you need to cover up a large area.

Cutting Tools

You'll need a small pair of scissors, plus a cutting knife and a metal ruler to guide it. Knives with retractable blades are safest. Discard dull blades, which might tear what you're cutting. Paper cutters are a great help at times and can be found at most copy shops.

Glue

Stick glue dries quickly, doesn't leave lumps, and is perfect for gluing down edges of paper.

Tape

You'll use Scotch tape instead of glue when working with transparencies. Scotch Magic tape, dull rather than shiny, won't be picked up by the copier.

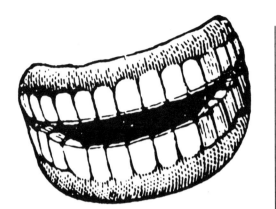

Finding Artwork

You've decided that you want a pterodactyl on your copier-made stationery. You draw one, but you're afraid the result might be mistaken for a pelican, or a flying clothespin. What do you do? You find a much better drawing of one, and copy it.

Tracking down art is detective work. It's fun and will often lead you to the library. As a deer knows the forest, you'll soon know the path to the card catalog or computer and from there the way to any book you may need. In the case of the pterodactyl, you might head for a dictionary or encyclopedia in the reference section. If you don't care for the pterodactyls you find there, you'd likely look up dinosaurs in the card catalog, jot down a call number or two, and find in those books many more pterodactyls from which to choose. Check for what you need in both the children's and adult sections. It feels good to know how to use the library and to find what you need on your own. And it's exciting when you set eyes on just the piece of artwork you want. You'll naturally need a library card so that you can check out the book and copy the artwork elsewhere if you want.

Photographs often don't copy very well. Much of the artwork you'll use will be old drawings and engravings.

These copy very clearly. They have another important advantage: They're old enough to be in the public domain—that is, copyright-free. This means that you can use them without permission from the publisher or artist. Clip art is art that is copyright-free. Any artwork originally published seventy-five years ago or more falls into this category. The doctrine of "fair use" most likely allows you to copy art from newer books as well as for the making of your own artwork. But if you plan to sell that artwork or use a large portion of a book in creating it, use only copyright-free art.

In Chapter 15 you'll find a list of books filled with art for copy artists. Libraries will have some of these books. The books published by Dover can often be bought at bookstores, art-supply stores, and stationery stores. Ask also at used-book stores, where the prices will be cheaper. Keep your eye out at garage sales and library book sales. Little by little, you can acquire your own library of artwork.

If you own a computer, you can buy disks of clip art. These cost much more than books but, like a home library, allow you to do much of your art searching at home.

Typefaces

Your copy art will often include words. Sometimes you'll want to write words out by hand. But much of the time you'll want them to look elegant or official or impressive. What do you do? Find a typewriter or computer. If you don't have one of these at home or at a friend's, your library might have public typewriters. Some copy shops have them; a few also have computers. They usually charge for each fifteen minutes or half hour.

You'll find the effect well worth the time. No matter how messy your handwriting, the words you type will be printed perfectly. You don't need to be an expert typist, though it's handy to know how to make corrections. What you've typed can then be enlarged or reduced on a copier, a feature many computer programs offer on their own. They usually offer as well a choice of typefaces in a variety of sizes. Electronic typewriters also allow you to use different typefaces by inserting different printwheels. But even the most ancient manual typewriter will do.

A B C D E F G H I J K
L M N O P Q R S T U
V W X Y Z 1 2 3 4 5 6 7

ABCDEFGHIJKLM NOPQRSTUV
abcdefghijklmnopqrstuvwxyz

Enlarging words a great deal leaves them rough-looking. For large letters, you might buy a sheet or two of transfer type at a stationery or art-supply store. These come in many sizes and styles, each with a supply of letters, numbers, and punctuation marks. Position the letter you want exactly where you want it, then rub it with the cap of a pen or other blunt tool. Magically, it will be transferred to your page. It's up to you to make sure that the letters are equally spaced and in a straight line. You can also buy sheets of lines, grids, and ornaments to be transferred.

AAaABCDEEFGHIJ
KKLMMMNNNOPQ
RRPSTTUVWXYZ

◆

abcdeffghhiijk
kklmmnnopqrstt
uvwxyz

◆

1234567890&.;!?

ABCDEFGHIJKLM
NOPQRSTUVWXYZ
abcdefghijklmn
opqrstuvwxyz

❖

1234567890?!:.;,"$&

ABCDEF
GHIJKL

ABCDEFG
HIJKLMN
OPQRSTU
VWXYZ&

.?.

ABCDEFG
HIJKLMN
OPQRSTU
VWXYZ
abcdefghij
klmnopqrs
tuvwxyz
12345678
90&;!?

12345678
MNOPQRSTUVWXYZ

Basic Techniques

Once you have mastered a few basic techniques, you will be ready to make all the projects in this book.

100%

Making Black-and-White Copies

Whatever it is that you're copying is called your original. Place it facedown on the copier's glass, lower the cover, and print.

● Make certain that what you want copied is on the part of the glass that the machine will "read." Ask if you're unsure.

● Avoid damaging the copier's glass with staples, paper clips, or whiteout that hasn't dried.

● When copying from a book, don't press down so hard that you hurt the book's spine.

● Legal-size paper works well for large originals or both pages of an opened book.

● If your original is in color, a black-and-white machine will convert the colors to black and various shades of gray.

● Don't forget to take your original when you're through.

Color Copies

There are two common types of color copiers: those that use a separate cartridge of ink for each color (single-color copiers) and laser copiers (which make full-color copies). Single-color copies are usually only a little more expensive than black and white. A black-and-white original will come out printed in red, blue, yellow, or whatever color you've chosen. At some shops, however, single-color copies are run on laser printers and cost as much as full color, often several dollars per page. Be sure to check prices.

● Color copies, especially full color, may take a little longer than black and white.

● Because color copies are more expensive, make sure your original is just the way you want it. This will save you paying for copies you're unhappy with.

● The quality of full-color copies varies. Take note of which shops' machines give the best results.

● If you've used a yellow pen to make guidelines, white out the lines before having your original copied. A color machine may pick up such lines.

70%

90%

60%

Reducing and Enlarging

Many machines allow you to change an image's size by various percentages. Normally, you'll find the machine set at 100 percent, meaning that the copy's image will be the same size as the original's. If you press the button for 125 percent, your copy's image will be 25 percent larger than your original's, or one quarter again as large. If you chose 75 percent, the copy's image will be 25 percent smaller than the original's, or three quarters the size.

● If your copy still isn't the size you'd like, you can use it as your original and reduce or enlarge the image further.

● Each time you make a copy from a copy, you lose darkness and detail. If you need something made extremely large or small, have this done behind the counter at a copy shop. The machine the clerk will use can accomplish this in fewer steps, giving you a more expensive but much sharper copy.

● When enlarging, you may need to copy onto legal-size or 11" x 17" paper to get the entire enlarged image on one sheet.

Darkening and Lightening

Many machines will let you vary the contrast or darkness of your copies.

● When copying an original on which you've done pasteup, too dark a setting will print the outlines of the paper you've glued down. These lines can, however, be whited out later.

● Too dark a setting will turn the white portion of your original to gray. This would be tedious to white out.

● If you need extremely dark copies (for example, silhouettes), have a copy-shop clerk print them behind the counter.

Cutting

● Small scissors are easier to handle than large ones.

● You needn't cut painstakingly close to the image you're cutting out in most cases.

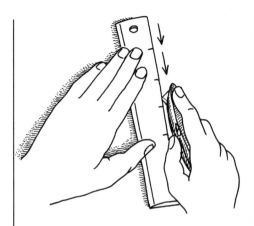

● When cutting with a knife, put heavy cardboard, a magazine, wood, or Plexiglas underneath.

● Surgeons use tools similar to yours. Always take care when using scissors or knives. Ask for adult help if you need it.

Pasteup

You'll often glue drawings and words from various sources onto one piece of paper. That paper will almost always be an 8½" x 11" sheet of white copy paper. If the piece you're gluing down is sticking up at all, the copier will print its edges as lines. A good pasteup job, with your additions' edges tightly affixed, will keep those unwanted lines off your copies. Tape picks up fingerprints and, if lifted, can tear the paper underneath or remove what's printed on it. Use stick glue except with transparencies.

● Turn your addition upside down on top of a piece of wastepaper. Move your glue stick around the entire edge, taking care not to crumple the paper. You won't need any glue in the middle.

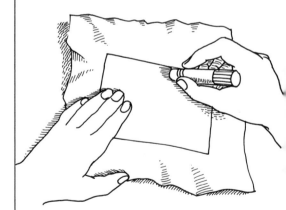

● Turn your addition right side up and place it where you want it. Try not to slide it around too much. Place a clean sheet of paper over it and rub with your palm. This will keep any glue on your hands off your paper.

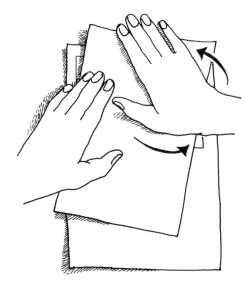

● If you need to draw guidelines to help you keep your additions straight or centered, use a yellow pen. Most copiers won't pick up this color, especially if your lines aren't heavy. If you're using a full-color copier (which will pick up yellow) you can always white out the lines after you've done your pasteup and no longer need them.

● Don't paste up anything within ¼ inch of the paper's edge. Many copiers don't pick up or print images there.

Whiting Out

● Shake the container of whiteout before you use it.

● Spread it in a thin coat. This will dry faster and won't leave you with crusty lumps, which are difficult to draw on, should you need to.

● Once the whiteout has dried, you can draw, type, and glue over

it. Ballpoint pens may work better than felt-tip here.

● Don't put paper on the copier's glass until any whiteout on it has dried.

Adding

Whiteout covers up what you don't want; with a pen or pencil, you can add what you do want.

● Try to match the art you're altering. If you want to add a hat to a finely etched head, use a fine-point pen.

● Consider sketching with a pencil first. It's easier to erase than to draw with a pen over layers of whiteout.

You might want to do some of these steps at home, where you may have more room to work, saving others for the copy shop or library. Planning what you'll do where and taking your kit of supplies along will cut down on the number of trips you'll need to make.

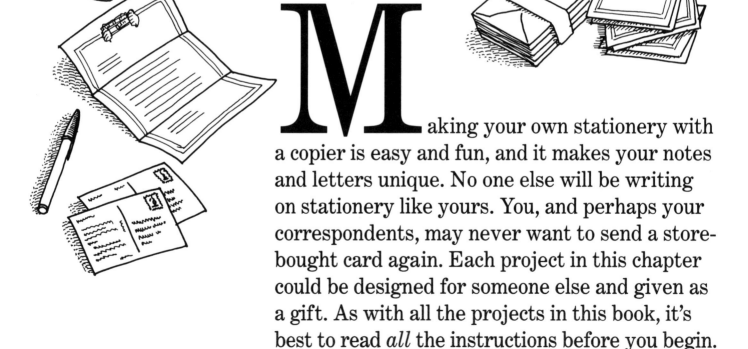

CHAPTER 1

Stationery

Making your own stationery with a copier is easy and fun, and it makes your notes and letters unique. No one else will be writing on stationery like yours. You, and perhaps your correspondents, may never want to send a store-bought card again. Each project in this chapter could be designed for someone else and given as a gift. As with all the projects in this book, it's best to read *all* the instructions before you begin.

Letterheads

These will be 8½" x 11" sheets of writing paper with your name and address.

Step 1.

Choose a Layout

Designing a letterhead, or anything else, is a matter of imagining all the possibilities you can and then choosing the one you like best. Do you like your name centered on the page or far to the left? How would it look to have the address centered under the name, or at the bottom of the page, or even sideways along one edge? There are no rules. Do some doodling, in your head or on paper.

In addition to various layouts, consider using transfer type, a border, adding an ornament or line, or using a drawing of something closely associated with you or where you live. This will make your letter head unmistakably yours.

Step 2.

Type

You'll probably want to type the name and address rather than use handwriting. Be sure to type onto white paper. Experiment with different typefaces, with capital letters (large) and lower case (small), and with adding spaces between the letters. Remember that you can enlarge what you've typed on a copier. If you're satisfied with your typewriter's typeface, you could type directly onto the 8½" x 11" sheet you'll use as your original.

N ɪ ᴄ ᴋ   J ᴏ ɴ ᴇ ꜱ

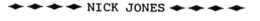

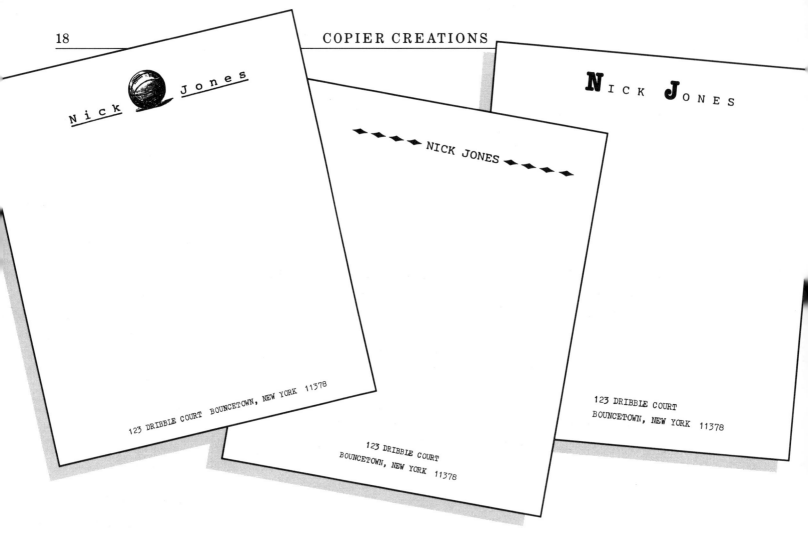

Step 3.

Pasteup

You're now ready to assemble your letterhead. Cut out the name and address you've decided on and any ornaments you'll be using. Arrange them on an 8½" x 11" sheet of white paper. How do they look? You might decide to alter your original design. Once you've made up your mind, you might want to use a ruler and yellow pen to measure and make guidelines that will keep your words straight or centered. Glue down everything in its place. If you're using transfer type, apply it after you've done your gluing. You're now ready to make copies.

Step 4.

Go to the Copy Shop

Look through the shop's paper samples. For only a few cents more than you'd pay for white copy paper, you can write your letters on paper that's regally heavy or Day-Glo bright. You can get ten sheets of one, five of another, and three of a third if you like. Keep in mind that writing will be harder to see on darker-colored sheets.

Once you've made your choice, the clerk will probably run off a proof and show it to you. This is your chance to see if any last-minute changes are needed. If your pasteup was done well, no outlines should show. If they do, the clerk will probably make another copy at a lighter setting. If this solves the problem but leaves the printing too light for your taste, white out the pasteup lines on the darker proof with copy-machine whiteout and use this as your original. White out any other marks or smudges you may not have noticed before. The clerk will then load the paper you asked for—and out will come your stationery.

Another Possibility

☞ If your letters don't often require a full sheet, consider getting two sheets of writing paper out of each 8½" x 11" sheet. Divide your original in half with a yellow pen to get two 5½" x 8½" sheets. These could be identical or different. Use a paper cutter to cut your finished copies in half. You'll be getting twice as many sheets of letterhead for your money.

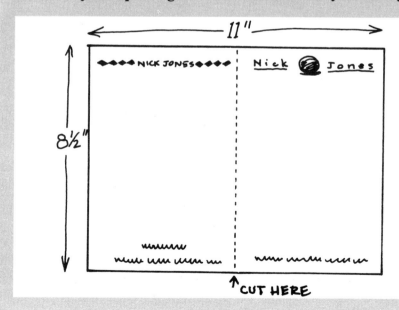

Notecards

Notecards are just right for thank-you's, invitations, or any brief message.

Step 1.
Lay Out Your Original

Turn an 8½" x 11" sheet of copy paper sideways and divide it with a yellow pen as shown. (If you divided the sheet exactly into quarters, your notecards would need an unusual and expensive size of envelope.) You'll glue your art to the lower portions, do some cutting and folding, and get two notecards per sheet that will fit into standard 6⅜" x 3⅝" envelopes.

Step 2.
Choose Your Artwork

There are no bounds to what you can put on your notecards. Look through books of clip art or any books on topics that interest you. You may need to reduce or enlarge. Some possibilities:

● A photo of you

● A drawing you've made

● A clip art drawing of an animal you like

● Part of a map that includes your area

● A dinosaur walking over a map that includes your area

● A poem you've written about a dinosaur walking down your street

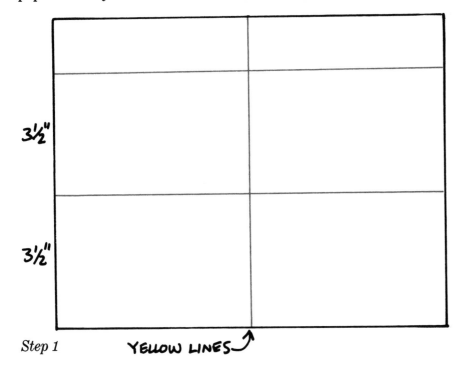

Step 1   YELLOW LINES

Step 3.

Design the Card and Paste It Up

Once you've found your art and copied it, you're ready to paste up your notecards. Remember:

● Since you'll be cutting the sheet in two, it's best to design your cards so that nothing is printed near where you'll be cutting. This way, if your cut is slightly off, you won't end up with a thin strip of one card's art on the other card.

● Your two cards could be identical (paste one up, make a copy, and glue that copy beside its mate). Or they could be different. Experiment. Make your own proof and see if you're getting the effect you want. Don't forget about lines and borders—your own, drawn with a pen and ruler, or fancier ones from clip art books.

Step 4.

Go to the Copy Shop

Now you get to pick out your paper. Notecards on card stock have a nice feel to them. This heavy paper costs a little more, but still far less than cards you'd buy at a store, especially since you'll be getting two per sheet. Check a proof before the cards are printed.

Step 5.

Cut and Fold

The finished cards will need two cuts. First, trim off the top 1½ inches so that the cards' two flaps will be the same size. Then cut the cards in half vertically. A paper cutter is much faster and more accurate than a knife and ruler, but more dangerous. Lastly, fold the cards and they're ready to send.

Another Possibility

☞ You could lay out your original on legal-size paper and get three slightly smaller cards per sheet. Find out if there's a nearby copy shop with legal-size card stock.

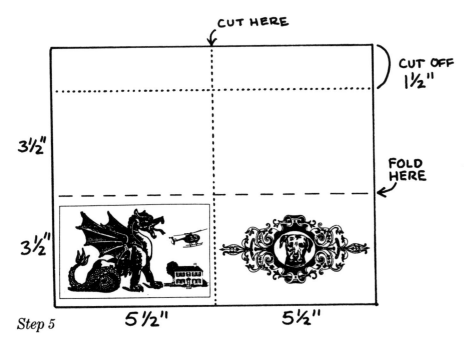

Step 5

Postcards

Postcards are easy to make and fun to receive. Because you can get four from each sheet of card stock, they're extremely inexpensive as well. Postal regulations require that they be at least 3½ x 5 inches. Cards larger than 4¼ x 6 inches will cost extra to send.

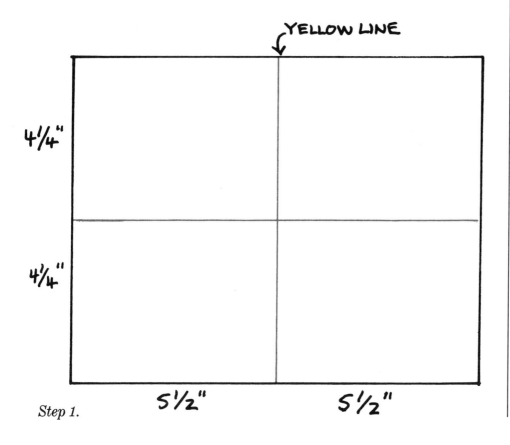

YELLOW LINE

4¼"

4¼"

5½"   5½"

Step 1.

Step 1.

Lay Out Your Original

Divide an 8½" x 11" sheet of copy paper with a yellow pen as shown, giving you four identical quarters. As on store-bought postcards, one side will have art and the other will be used for both the address and your message.

Step 2.

Choose and Copy Your Art

Use your imagination. Some possibilities:

● An amusing photo or drawing

● A realistic caption typed in at the bottom, just as on real postcards

● A famous monument altered (your photo added to the heads on Mount Rushmore, etc.)

● A made-up tourist attraction ("Giant Umbrella Mushroom Caves")

Possibilities for Step 2.

Greetings

Step 3.

Pasteup

You could paste up four different cards on your original, or four identical cards. Lines and borders are very effective on postcards. Remember too that you can add transfer type on top of other artwork—something often seen on postcards. Since you'll be cutting your printed sheets into quarters, don't glue anything right up to the lines or closer than ⅛ inch from the paper's edge.

Step 4.

Go to the Copy Shop

Any paper lighter in weight than card-stock will likely get bent on its trip through the mail. Find out which shop has the colors you like best. If that shop is inconveniently far, you can buy a supply of blank sheets from them to use, as needed, closer to home. Check a proof before you have your postcards printed.

Step 5.

Cut

Cut the finished card-stock sheets in half in both directions. The clerk might do this for you without charge at some shops. Your postcards are now ready for your pen.

CUT HERE

CUT HERE

POSTCARD	POSTCARD
To	To
POSTCARD	POSTCARD
To	To

Step 5.

Second Annual Piggyback Jump

Camp Scratchit

PUMPKIN PIE TIME

Other Possibilities

☞ Homemade postcards have been made by many artists. Find the books on mail art listed in the *Recommended Books* section. By sending out your postcards, you can join a network of mail artists and begin receiving their postcards in your mailbox. Use your cards to invite your friends to send you their copier-made cards. You'll get lots of new ideas this way.

☞ Make your postcards look even more "real" by printing lines for the name and address, a box for the stamp, a dividing line, etc., on the *back* of the card. Look at several postcards to get ideas. This requires making a second original and putting your sheets of cards through the machine a second time. This is called double-sided copying. Print a proof to make sure that both sides are aligned and facing in the right direction.

☞ After you've read some of the other chapters in this book, you might want to go back and apply to stationery what you learned about silhouettes, color, overlapping, and transparencies.

CHAPTER • 2

Silhouettes

S ilhouettes were executed by ancient Egyptian stonecarvers and Greek vase painters. In the eighteenth and nineteenth centuries, silhouette cutters roamed Europe and America, snipping their sitters' portraits from black paper. With the invention of the camera, silhouettes all but disappeared. The copy machine, however, makes it easy for you to continue this venerable art, and to make copies of any size easily.

Step 1.

Trace the Subject's Outline

Two people are needed—a subject and a tracer. Seat the subject next to a wall to which you've taped a blank piece of 11" x 17" copy paper. You can buy these sheets at a copy shop. Position a lamp a few feet away, level with the subject's head. If you remove the lamp's shade, you'll get a sharper silhouette. Experiment with the placement of the lamp and paper until the subject's whole profile is cast on the paper. The subject will need to be quite close to the paper and old enough to be able to sit very still for a minute or so. The tracer copies the shadow's outline onto the paper with a black pen. Be especially careful when tracing the features of the face.

Step 2.

Reduce the Outline

By reducing, you can make your silhouette as small as you like. You could, of course, leave it life size. If you want to reduce it, roll up your sheet and take it to a copy shop. Because of its size, you may need to have a clerk reduce it. The more you reduce, the easier it will be to fill in the outline later. You can always have the inked-in silhouette enlarged later if you wish.

Step 3.

Fill in the Outline

Once you have the size of outline you want, fill it in with black ink. A black Magic Marker works well with large silhouettes. Use a finer-point pen when you come to the eyes and nose and mouth, since a slip here could make the silhouette look like someone else's.

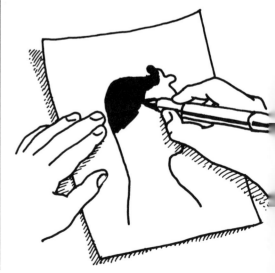

Step 4.

Make Copies

Have this done behind the copy shop's counter, so as to get the darkest silhouettes possible. You can have them made on any weight or color of paper. If you've kept your silhouette very large, you might only be able to make copies onto white, since 11" x 17" paper is often unavailable in colors and heavier weights. Consider having your silhouette reduced or enlarged to other sizes. Be sure to check a proof. Even some behind-the-counter machines don't produce large solid black areas well.

Step 5.

Trim

With a paper cutter or knife, trim your copies so that the silhouettes are in the middle of the paper.

Step 6.

Mount

You can put up your silhouette or give it away as a gift just as it is. Or you could go to an art-supply or stationery store, where inexpensive mats for framing are often sold. These come in many colors and sizes. Slipping your silhouette behind one of these and affixing it with a touch of glue will display it in striking fashion.

Other Possibilities

☞ Add a border around the silhouette. You can draw your own or find one you like in a clip art book. Reduce or enlarge it to size, cut it out, and glue it around your inked-in silhouette.

☞ Make a double silhouette. Trace your silhouette and someone else's on two separate sheets. After reducing, glue the outlines facing each other (or however you want them), ink them in, and make copies. Be sure you've reduced them to the same size.

☞ Have your silhouette copied onto your letterhead, notecards, or postcards.

☞ Many old-time silhouette cutters made negative silhouettes, in which the head is white and the background black. You can do this by inking in *around* the outline you've traced instead of inside it. Be sure to ink

in up to where you plan to trim. Some copy shops can print reversals, making everything that's white on your original come out black on the copy. This would allow you to get both types of silhouettes from the

same original. Check the price first. Intricate borders look especially nice printed white-on-black—as lacy as spider webs.

☞ Try casting other shadows on the paper to trace: hands, dolls, masks, etc. If the object is

flat, you could trace around it rather than around its shadow.

☞ Copy a drawing from a clip art book and ink it in, turning it into a silhouette.

☞ Rather than filling in your subject's outline, try having it copied just as it is, reduced to the size you want. The line will become very fine if you reduce it a great deal; you may want to go over it with a heavier pen. Consider having a reversal of this made, giving you a white outline against a black background.

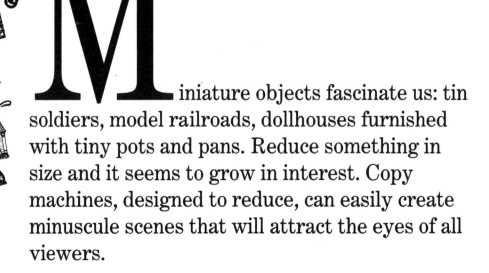

CHAPTER • 3

Miniatures

Miniature objects fascinate us: tin soldiers, model railroads, dollhouses furnished with tiny pots and pans. Reduce something in size and it seems to grow in interest. Copy machines, designed to reduce, can easily create minuscule scenes that will attract the eyes of all viewers.

A Street Scene

You can create your own miniaturized city block, peopled with whom—or what—you decide to include. By making several copies, you can expand this tiny scene into an entire city.

Step 1.

Lay Out Your Original

With a yellow pen, divide an 8½" x 11" sheet of copy paper as shown. Make a mark with a black pen near the end of each yellow line; these will guide you when you cut out the strips later.

Step 2.

Find Your Artwork

You'll fill the five 1½-inch strips you've laid out with buildings, people, cars, animals, trees, parades, and anything else that might come down a street. Look through clip art books. Figures in action will make your street come alive: peddlers calling, dogs running, fire engine clanging. Look for drawings of buildings seen from the front rather than at an angle.

Step 3.

Copy Your Artwork

At the library or copy shop, copy the artwork you've chosen. Bring along your original so that you'll know how much you need to reduce it. The figures shouldn't touch the yellow lines. If a lot of reducing is required, you might paste up several pieces of art on

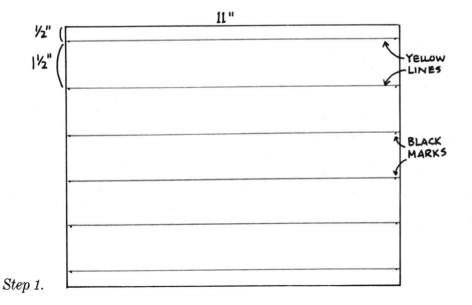

Step 1.

Step 4.

a single sheet and have a copy-shop clerk reduce it. This will save some money and give you much clearer copies.

Step 4.
Pasteup

Do this step where little bits of art won't get lost or blown off a table. You'll want small scissors and may need to trim closely around your figures. You'll have fun deciding what goes where. You may decide to go back for more artwork. Don't glue any figures outside the black marks you made.

Step 5.
Copy and Assemble

Look over your original for any last-minute whiting out or adding. Then have it copied onto card stock at a copy shop. If the yellow lines show up on the proof, white them out on the original (or on the proof, if that's easier). Don't white out the black marks, however. Cut the printed sheets into strips, using the black marks as your guide and trimming them off afterward. Tape the strips together into long streets, square blocks, or circular avenues. Each sheet of card stock

will give you almost five feet of street to display on a shelf or table or play with on the floor. Supports from folded pieces of card stock will keep long street scenes upright.

Other Possibilities

☞ If your copy shop has legal-size card stock, you can lay out your original on this size of paper and get even longer strips and more street scene per page.

☞ Make enough copies to be able to assemble an entire city on the floor, with branching streets, dead ends, etc.

☞ Instead of a city scene, make a country scene with hills, woods, grazing animals, etc.

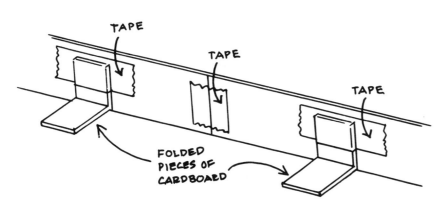

TAPE

TAPE

TAPE

FOLDED PIECES OF CARDBOARD

Step 5.

A Folding House

This house can easily be mailed to friends, who'll have fun putting it together. It makes a nice Christmas ornament, as well.

Step 1.

Copy the Layout and Artwork

Make a copy of the house plan on p. 39 onto white copy paper. Then search for some residents in clip art books. As on a stage set, you'll see "through" the walls and into the house. You have eight rooms to fill with diners, dogs, cardplayers, musicians, children, readers, or whomever you like. Silhouettes look quite striking when reduced. You'll probably need to do a lot of reducing, and you may want to have a copy-shop clerk do it. Take the house plan along so that you'll know when you've got your family down to the right size.

Step 2.

Pasteup

Glue your artwork where you want it. With a black pen you could add shutters around the upper windows, hanging lamps, or other details.

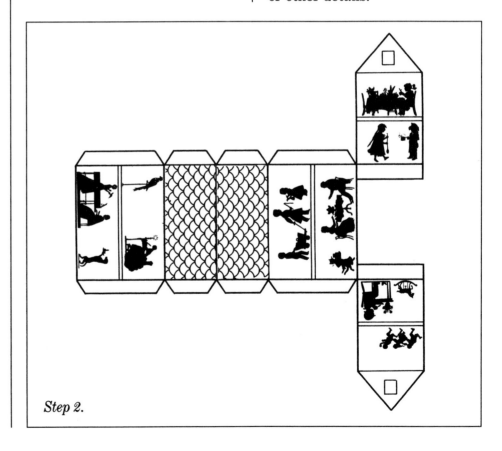

Step 2.

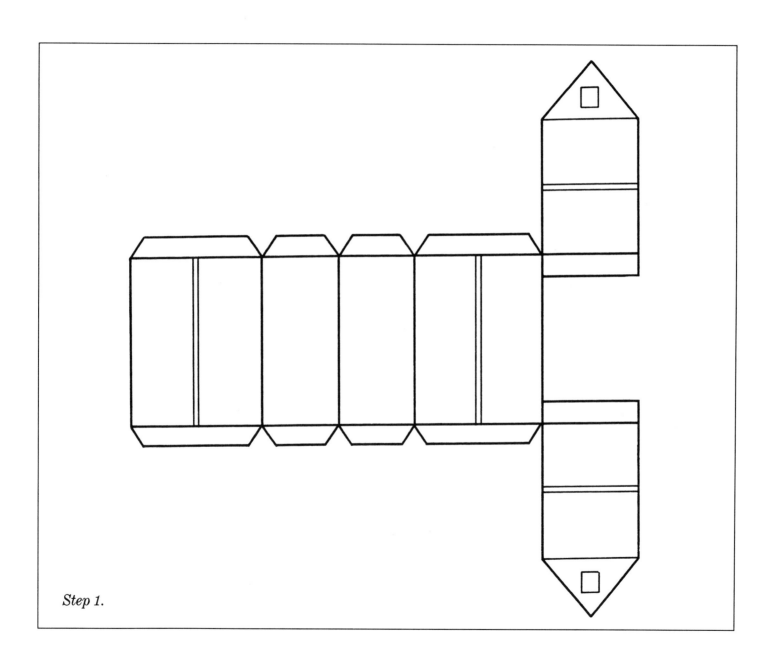

Step 1.

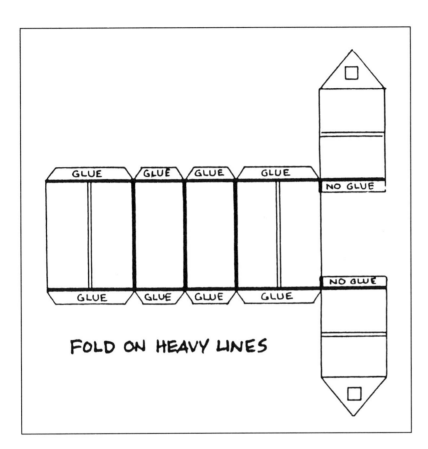

GLUE GLUE GLUE GLUE

NO GLUE

NO GLUE

GLUE GLUE GLUE GLUE

FOLD ON HEAVY LINES

Step 3.
Make Copies

Go to a copy shop and make copies onto card stock. You might try several different colors.

Step 4.
Cut and Assemble

With a small pair of scissors cut out the house. Then turn it print side down and fold *upward* on the lines indicated on p. 40. A ruler and butter knife or similar objects work well for this. The side of the house with the narrow rooms gets folded in two directions so as to swing up into place. Spread a thick coat of stick glue on one tab at a time, fold it into place, and attach it, reaching inside the house with one hand and pressing tightly with your fingers. Your house is now ready to sit on your desk or a windowsill, or to hang by a thread from a Christmas tree.

Other Possibilities

☞ By having your original reduced to various percentages when it's printed onto card stock, you can make houses of various sizes. By pasting up several different houses, you could put together a street of houses, each a different size and color and with a different scene inside.

☞ Try designing your own house plan. You might use a flat roof instead of a peaked one. Consider dividing the house into more floors and smaller rooms, with even smaller people inside. Try making a house that's long and low, or an apartment building that's tall and narrow. Using 11" x 17" paper will give you more possibilities. Some copy shops carry card stock in this size.

☞ For houses you'll be sending to others, you might want to make a much-reduced copy of the house, showing where to fold and glue. This could be squeezed onto your original and copied onto card stock beside the house.

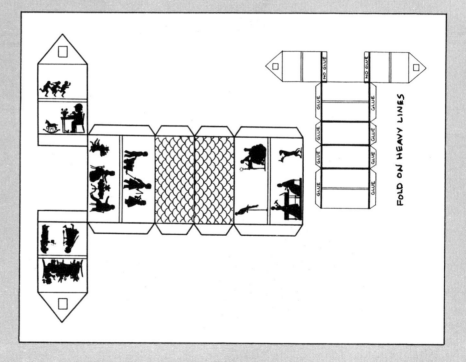

CHAPTER • 4

Jigsaw Puzzles

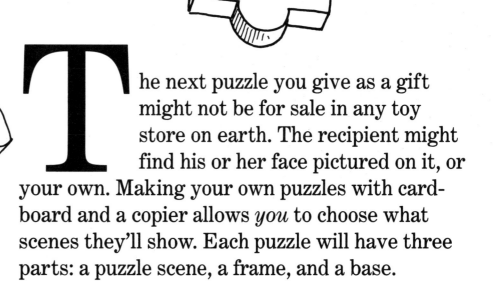

The next puzzle you give as a gift might not be for sale in any toy store on earth. The recipient might find his or her face pictured on it, or your own. Making your own puzzles with cardboard and a copier allows *you* to choose what scenes they'll show. Each puzzle will have three parts: a puzzle scene, a frame, and a base.

Step 1.

Copy Your Scene

There's no limit to what you might put on your puzzle. A few possibilities:

- A drawing you've done

- A clip art drawing of an animal or activity or place you like

- The page from the phone book listing the person you'll give the puzzle to

- A photo of your face, or of the face of the person you'll give it to

● A scene that would make a puzzle difficult to solve (a detailed map, a complex design, a page of text in a foreign language)

Once you've decided on a scene, copy it, reducing or enlarging it to the size you want. If there's unwanted artwork on the page, cut out what you want, glue it to a new sheet, and have it copied again.

If you're using a photo, have it copied behind the copy shop's counter, where there's likely to be a machine that has a setting designed for photographs. It's best to bring in a print, either color or black and white, though some copy shops can make copies from slides and negatives.

If the scene you've chosen is in color, consider having it copied in full color. Although this is expensive, you'll need only one copy. If you want to make several puzzles, you could make them small and get several puzzles' worth of scenes on each color copy. If your original is black and white, you might want to have it copied in blue, red, or one of the other colors available on a single-color machine.

Step 2.

Draw a Box

With a ruler and a regular pencil, draw a box around your scene. This will be the puzzle pieces' outer edges. Making this edge straight, rather than curved, will make your cutting much easier. With scissors, cut around your box, cutting ½ inch or so to the outside of your lines.

Step 2.

CUT ½ INCH OR SO OUTSIDE OF BOX. (SHOWN HERE AS A DOTTED LINE.)

Step 3.
Get Materials

There are several different materials you can make your puzzle from. Whichever you choose, get a piece that's big enough to lay your scene on in three different places with an inch of space in between. This will give you enough room to make the puzzle, the puzzle frame, and the base.

Cardboard works fine for puzzles. Find a smooth, flat sheet about ⅟₁₆ inch thick. If it's thicker, with large air spaces in the middle, it will be difficult to cut the scene into puzzle pieces without bending the edges. If it's thinner, the puzzle pieces may curl and slip out of the frame.

You might buy a sheet of poster board at a stationery store. It's inexpensive and comes in many colors, giving you an attractive puzzle frame. Try to find some that's ⅟₁₆ inch thick. Only slightly more expensive is foam-core board, which is thick (³⁄₁₆ inch) but easy to cut. This is

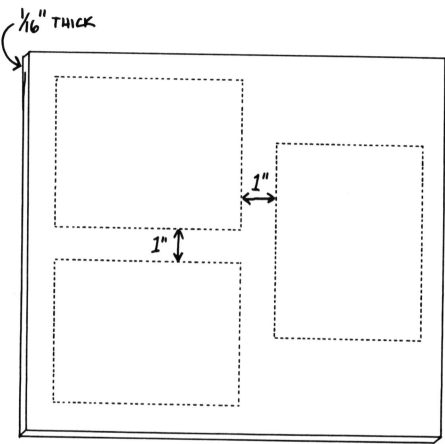

Step 3.

the best material to use. Puzzle pieces made from it are pleasingly thick and won't slip out of their frame. Foam-core board comes only in white and is sold at stationery and art-supply stores.

Step 4.
Make the Puzzle

Turn your boxed scene upside down and spread a heavy coat of glue on the *entire* surface. Then

GLUE IMAGE TO CARDBOARD AND CUT ALONG LINES OF BOX.

Step 4.

glue it down to one corner of your cardboard, covering it with a clean sheet of paper and rubbing with your palm back and forth.

Once the glue has dried, you're ready to cut. Since scissors tend to bend cardboard and cause creases, you'll use a cutting knife for all the cutting in this project. Take your knife and a metal ruler, put something underneath the cardboard to protect your work surface, hold the ruler down tightly, and cut along the box you drew. You'll probably need to run your knife along the ruler several times. Remove the puzzle from the surrounding cardboard sheet and erase any pencil marks on it.

Step 5.
Make the Frame

The frame will keep the puzzle from sliding off the base. If you want it to be 1 inch wide on all sides, take your puzzle and lay it

on another part of the cardboard where there's at least 1 inch of cardboard around it. Trace around the puzzle with a regular pencil. Then take a ruler and make the box you've just drawn just a hair wider and taller (no more than 1/16 inch). This will give the puzzle pieces a tiny bit of room to move around.

Cut out this enlarged box with your ruler and knife. To keep cut marks from showing on the finished frame, start at each corner and cut toward the middle, following the lines you've drawn so that the two cuts meet cleanly. Remove the piece of cardboard

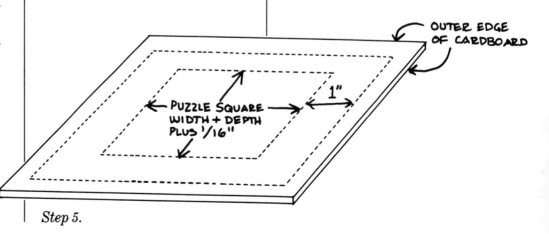

OUTER EDGE OF CARDBOARD

PUZZLE SQUARE WIDTH + DEPTH PLUS 1/16"

1"

Step 5.

you've just cut out.

Next, take your ruler, measure 1 inch beyond each side of the opening (or however wide you want your frame to be), and draw the lines of the frame's outer edge. Then cut along the lines using your knife and ruler. Remove the frame and erase any pencil marks. You've finished the hardest part of puzzle making.

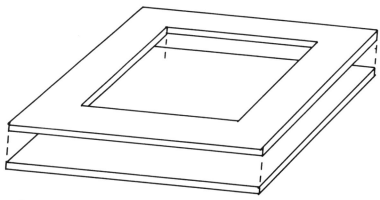

Step 7.

Step 6.
Make the Base

Lay the frame on your cardboard. Trace around the frame's *outer* edge with a regular pencil.

Use your knife and ruler to cut along these lines. You've just cut out the puzzle's base. Remove the base, which should be the same size as the frame but without an opening in the middle.

Step 7.
Glue Down the Frame

Spread a heavy coat of glue on the entire back of the frame, then set it down on the base. Press them firmly together.

Step 8.
Cut Up the Puzzle

The final step is the most fun. Taking your knife, cut the puzzle into pieces. Sweeping curves are satisfying to execute, but try to keep your knife blade straight up

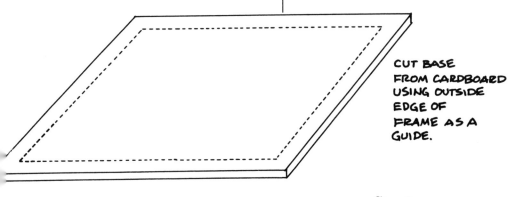

CUT BASE FROM CARDBOARD USING OUTSIDE EDGE OF FRAME AS A GUIDE.

Step 6.

and down rather than at an angle. Avoid starting and stopping during a cut. When you've finished, assemble the pieces in the frame. After working the puzzle yourself, you might decide to cut some of the pieces into smaller pieces.

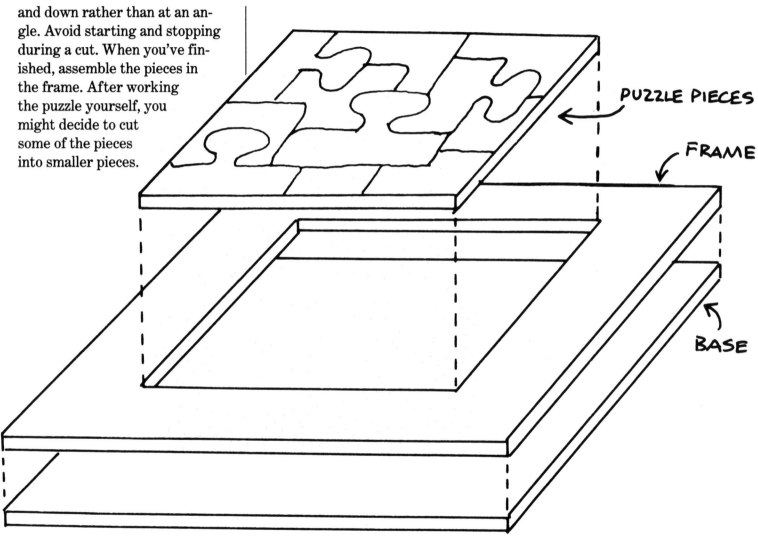

Step 8.

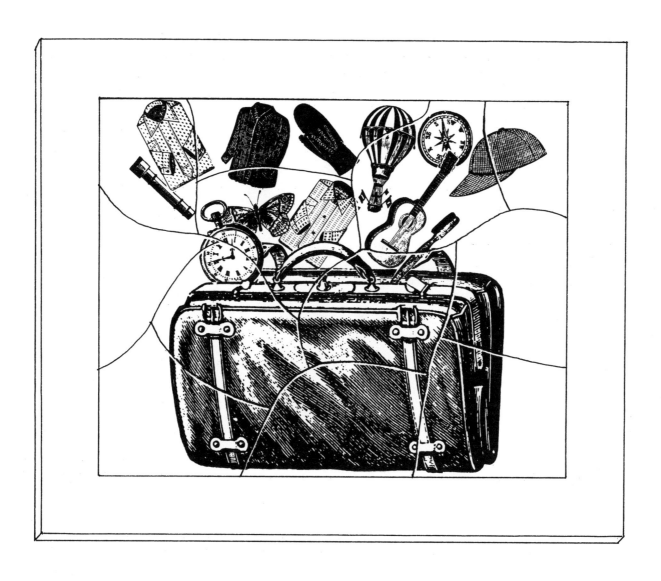

Other Possibilities

☞ Use transfer type to add ornaments or words to your frame—perhaps the name of the person or place or thing pictured.

☞ Make a double puzzle by gluing art to *both* sides of your puzzle. Make a copy of two scenes you want to use. In Step 2, draw a box around just one of them. In Step 4, after gluing that scene down and cutting out the puzzle, use the puzzle to trace a box around the second scene. Cut along that box and glue the second scene onto the puzzle's other side. Then follow Steps 5 through 8.

☞ Consider gluing artwork to the base in Step 6. If your puzzle shows the face of an adult, you might copy a photo of the subject as a baby and glue it to the portion of the base that shows when the puzzle's pieces are removed. Your puzzle's recipient will get a double surprise.

☞ Cutting the frame can be difficult. You can save some time and trouble by buying a mat at an art-supply or stationery store. These are inexpensive and come in many sizes and colors. Reduce or enlarge your scene with the mat's opening in mind. In Step 2 use this opening to trace the box around your artwork; in this case, you'll then need to *reduce* the size of this box by a tiny amount on two sides before you cut. The cardboard you use for the puzzle shouldn't be thicker than the mat. Skip Step 5. Many mats come with a base, allowing you to skip step 6 as well. If yours didn't, use the mat's outer edge to trace the shape of the base in Step 6.

CHAPTER 5

Decals

Y ou've seen them on cars everywhere—decals certifying the driver's visit to the Okefenokee Swamp, her attendance at the Gilroy, California, Garlic Festival, his membership in the Friends of the Sea Otter. And yet, without traveling any farther than a copy shop, you can outdo the owner of the most decal-laden RV by producing your own decals on transparencies.

About Transparencies

Decals are made by copying onto sheets of clear plastic, the sort that teachers use with overhead projectors. These are usually known as transparencies, although some copy shops might call them acetate or drafting film. They're usually only available in 8½" x 11" size and come plain or with a peel-off sticky back. They're loaded in the machine just like paper, can have black or colors copied onto them, and are easy to cut with scissors or a knife. They're also much more durable than paper. You can use whiteout on them (the side with the whiteout must be facedown on the glass when you make a copy from the transparency). You can also draw on them, using a black pen made for marking photographs. Some transparencies have a white strip along one edge. If possible, use those with a strip that peels off or those with no strip at all.

Although transparencies cost more than paper, they offer the copy artist myriad possibilities. The projects in this chapter and chapters 6 and 10 all make use of them.

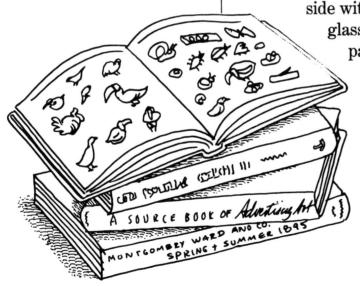

A SOURCE BOOK OF *Advertising Art*

MONTGOMERY WARD AND CO. SPRING + SUMMER 1895

Step 2.
Copy Your Artwork

Search out the art you'll need. Often you'll want to make alterations: whiting out this, adding in that, reducing, combining bits and pieces from several sources. Should you want a particular drawing reversed in direction (a hand pointing left instead of right), a transparency can do this for you. Simply have the artwork copied onto one, then use the transparency as your original, placing it faceup on the copy machine to produce the reversed image on a copy. This is a handy technique to know whenever you're gathering artwork for a project.

Step 1.
Choose a Subject

Your decals can picture any place, holiday, group—real or imaginary—that you like. Look at decals on cars to get ideas. Some possibilities:

● A place you've actually visited

● A place no one has visited (the center of the earth, Neptune, etc.)

● An imaginary celebration or organization

● A made-up monument

● A personal statement ("Eat More Sturgeon")

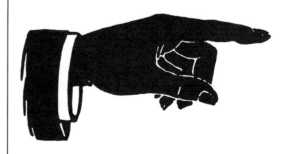

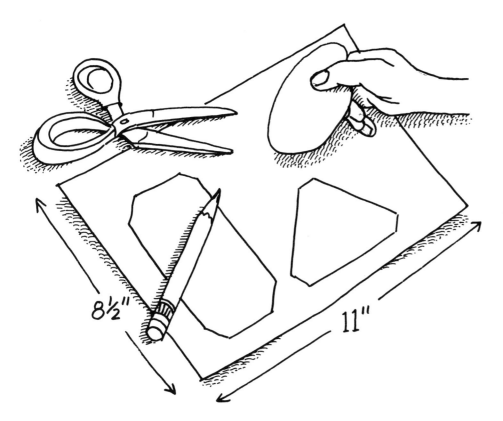

8½"

11"

Step 3.
Lay Out Your Original

Decide what size and shape you want your decal to be. A border often makes decals stand out. You can draw your own or find one you like in a clip art book.

Since decals usually have words, think about where you want them to go. You can use transfer type to superimpose them over your artwork, or they can be pasted up along your border or elsewhere.

If you want to make more than one type of decal, you can paste up or draw in more borders on your sheet, leaving at least ½ inch between them.

Step 4.
Produce Your Words

You now should have a good idea what size you want your words to be. Using a typewriter or transfer type for your words will do wonders toward making your decal look authentic.

If you're using a typewriter, type your words on a separate sheet of paper; that way, if you make a mistake you won't have ruined your decal original. Before typing, see how much room you have for your letters on the decal. You could measure this and make a line of that length on the page you're typing on. Using that line as a guide, you might find you have room to put a space (or two or three) between the letters. You might type some words in all capital letters, and others in capitals and lower case. Experiment. If you can, try more than one typeface. You can always enlarge or reduce what you've typed. Larger and heavier letters will be more easily read.

Live Bug Club
Live Bug Club
LIVE BUG CLUB
L I V E   B U G   C L U B
Live Bug Club
LIVE BUG CLUB

If you're using transfer type, you can press the letters right onto your original. There are dozens of different typefaces to choose from. Make sure the sheet you use has enough of each letter you'll need. If it doesn't, you can always copy the sheet and glue down, rather than transfer, the needed letter. This won't work, however, if you're superimposing the letters over artwork. If you don't have a border to guide you, use a yellow pen to draw a guideline to keep your letters straight. Gauge in advance how much space you'll leave between them before you begin.

Step 5.
Pasteup

Cut out your art and words and glue them onto your original. If you want to superimpose transfer type on your art, do this after the art is pasted up.

Step 6.
Make Your Final Original

You can save money and get more decals in the bargain by having your original copied several times onto copy paper, cutting out the decals, and pasting them up on a new original. This way you may be able to get five or six (or as many as you can fit) on each transparency you pay for. You might want someone to reduce them at this point. Have this

copying done behind the counter, to keep the copies sharp. Check them as you would a proof. When you do your gluing, arrange the decals so as to get as many on the page as possible. Leave at least ½ inch between them.

Your final original might have six copies of the same decal or six completely different ones. Or you might have three different decals and three copies of another you particularly like.

If you want your decals printed in black or a single color, go to Step 7.

For more money, you'll get a lot of effect by having your decals made in full color. Make several black-and-white copies of your final original. You'll use these to experiment on. Then take out your felt pens and add color to your decals, the same way you'd color in a page of a coloring book. You can color right over words and artwork, as long as the color isn't too dark. Wide-tipped highlighting pens work well for filling in large areas, and their pastel shades won't obscure your art or words. Try various colors and combinations until you've got a final original that's colored just the way you want it.

Step 7.

Copy onto Transparencies

Take your final original to a copy shop and have it copied onto a transparency or onto several. You might have one made in black and one or more in single colors. If you're having your decals made in full color, you may want to ask for a light setting if you think some of the colors may obscure words or artwork underneath. A copy's colors are often deeper than those on your original.

Step 8.

Cut and Put on Glass

Cut out your decals with scissors or a knife and ruler. There should be enough space between them to allow you to cut ¼ inch or so outside of the decals' borders.

At last you're ready to put them on. They'll last longer if you put them on the inside of the window, protected from the elements. Clean and dry the glass you'll be sticking them to. You'll need some glue that dries clear, available at stationery or art-supply stores.

Spread it all over the front of the decal, then press and hold the decal against the glass. Once the glue dries, use a sponge and water to remove any glue that squeezed out beneath the decal. You can also use Scotch tape to attach the decals, though the edges of the tape will show.

Your car, house, or suitcase is now a work of art!

Other Possibilities

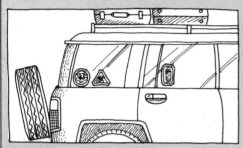

☞ Exchange decals with friends or other copy artists to increase your collection.

☞ Consider documenting an actual family vacation through a series of homemade decals.

☞ If you want your decals to be much more noticeable, copy them onto paper or card stock, choosing from the many colors available. You needn't pay for full-color copying: Simply have them copied in black, then add color to them with felt pens. Because glue shows on paper (as it doesn't on transparencies), use tape to attach them to your window. Keep them on the small side, since you won't be able to see through them out the window as you can through transparencies.

☞ To avoid having to glue your decals on, you could have them printed on sticky-back transparencies. These are handy for decals you'll be sending to other people, who can then peel off the backing and put them right on. Sticky backs,

however, often don't adhere as well as glued decals. They'll also need to go on the outside of the window, and they can't be copied in full color. Try a sheet of both plain and sticky-back transparencies and see which you like better.

CHAPTER • 6

Multiple Images

Not only can a copy machine make many copies of one original—it can combine many originals into a single copy. This is called superimposing images. If you put two or more transparencies on the glass (and a paper original, if you like), your copy will carry all their images. You can get the same effect by making a copy of one image, then placing that copy in the machine's paper tray and copying a second image (and a third, and a fourth) on top of it. The possibilities are endless. Here are just a few of them.

A Double Portrait

C opiers allow you to make portraits with two or more superimposed subjects.

Step 1.
Find Your Artwork

Take a silhouette of a head, place a piece of tracing paper on top of it, and trace the outline with a heavy-tipped black pen. If you can find a photo of the subject taken in profile, you could trace the outline from that. Reduce or enlarge what you've traced if you wish.

Next, find a piece of art showing something associated with your subject: a musical instrument, a particular landmark or landscape, the map of a state or city, a football, etc. The darker the image, the harder it will be to see the face you'll print over it. Copy the art,

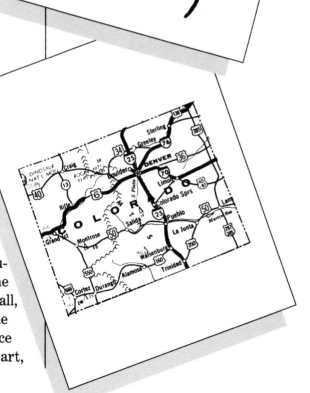

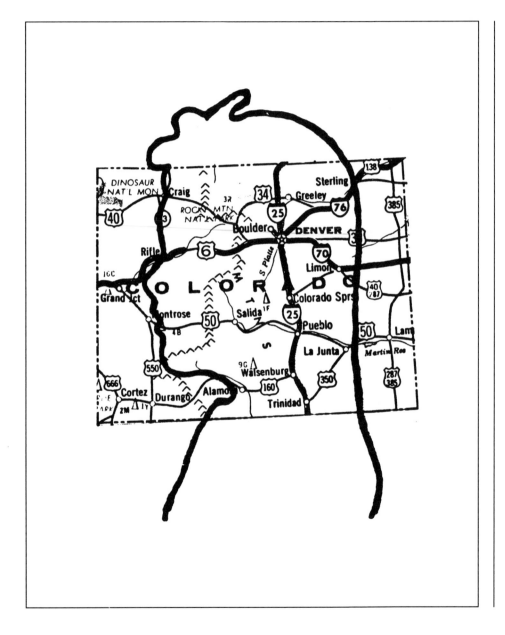

enlarging or reducing to the size you want, imagining it superimposed on the portrait. Cut out the image, glue it on its own sheet, do any whiting out or adding, and have a transparency made of it.

Step 2.

Superimpose the Images

Place the transparency over the face. Align the two as you want them, then tape two of the edges to hold them in place. If you press the tape down well, it shouldn't show. It doesn't matter if the two sheets' edges don't meet exactly.

Step 3.

Copy

Take this paper-and-transparency original to a copy shop and make copies. Check a proof. You might want to realign the images or white out part of the superimposed art. Take the

finished copies, trim them as desired, and your double portrait is finished.

This technique is handy whenever you're creating an original that calls for one image appearing on top of or in front of another. If you want to show a giant fly on the face of the Mona Lisa, it would be very difficult to cut out those thin legs with their tiny hairs. A transparency of the fly, taped in place, will give you every detail with none of the scissor work. Since the transparency is clear, the background art will show through if your superimposed art is mainly outline. To remedy this, you can do some careful whiting out of the background art before making the transparency, or fill in your superimposed art, making it a solid silhouette.

Other Possibilities

☞ Try superimposing two portraits facing each other, overlapping halfway.

☞ Superimpose on a present-day scene a scene from the past: a residential scene and an Indian camp, a city scene and dinosaurs, etc.

☞ Superimpose the silhouettes of migrating birds onto a map.

A Time-Exposure Scene

Aphotographer makes a time exposure by leaving the camera's shutter open longer than usual, allowing the film to record the motion of subjects. You've probably seen such photos of the movement of the stars or of cars' headlights at night. The copier can similarly compress comings and goings over a period of time into a single image. All you need do is copy several transparencies at once.

Step 1.

Copy Your Background

If you wish to show a day in the life of a city street, for example, find a street scene you like and copy it onto paper, reducing or enlarging it to roughly 4 x 9 inches. Glue it onto its own sheet of copy paper.

Step 2.
Create Your Foreground

Turn an 8½" x 11" sheet on its side and divide it into strips with a yellow pen as shown. Glue down onto these strips anything and everything that might pass down your street: fish sellers, buses, bicycles, rickshaws, cows, coaches. Glue them fairly close together, but leave 1 inch at the sides for taping. When you've finished, have this sheet copied onto a transparency.

¼"

2"

YELLOW
LINE

Step 3.

Superimpose and Copy

Cut the transparency into the four strips you pasted up. If you hold them together up to the light, you'll get a sense of what your final copy will look like. Place the strips, one on top of another, on the bottom half of your street scene. By turning the strips over, you can make your figures head in the opposite direction. Tape down both sides. Take this concoction to a copy shop. Your copies will seem to

produce a cacophony of honking, shouting, and mooing all by themselves.

Other Possibilities

☞ Picture the combined arrivals and departures of birds on a telephone wire.

☞ Create a dance floor crowded with dancers.

☞ Compress the action on a soccer or football field into a single image.

☞ Increase the number of combined images by using your finished copy as your new background scene and taping your transparencies to it.

Color Overlays

Y ou now know how to produce multiple images. Color copiers allow you to produce multiple colors as well by copying originals in various colors onto the same sheet of paper.

Color weavings are easy and fun, and offer unending possibilities through superimposing colors.

Step 1.
Create Your Patterns

Make two or more copies of a solid black square, drawing an arrow at the top of the page first. Take out your correction tape and mask out different areas of each square. Using different widths of correction tape will give further variety to your designs. Since the tape is easy to lift off the page and put down again, it's easy to experiment with different patterns. You could also use whiteout to make curves and other shapes.

Step 2.
Copy

Take your squares to a copy shop that has a single-color copier. You might have the first square printed in red. Then have that red copy loaded in the paper tray, have the clerk put your second square on the glass, and have it printed in a different color onto the red copy. Because the squares are in the identical place on each sheet, they'll be aligned on the finished weaving, as long as they're positioned in the same place on the copier's glass. Use the arrows at the tops of the pages to make sure each sheet faces in the same direction on the glass. You could continue this process, with a different square for as many colors as the machine offers. After three colors, however, the results often look muddy. Two colors, printed onto colored paper, offer plenty of color complication. If no single-color machine is available, a full-color machine will do the job and offer even more colors—but at a much higher price. Try using just black as well. The weaving effect will still come through, and will look good on colored paper. Since you'd just need a black-and-white copier, you could use a self-service machine and do it all yourself.

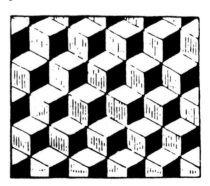

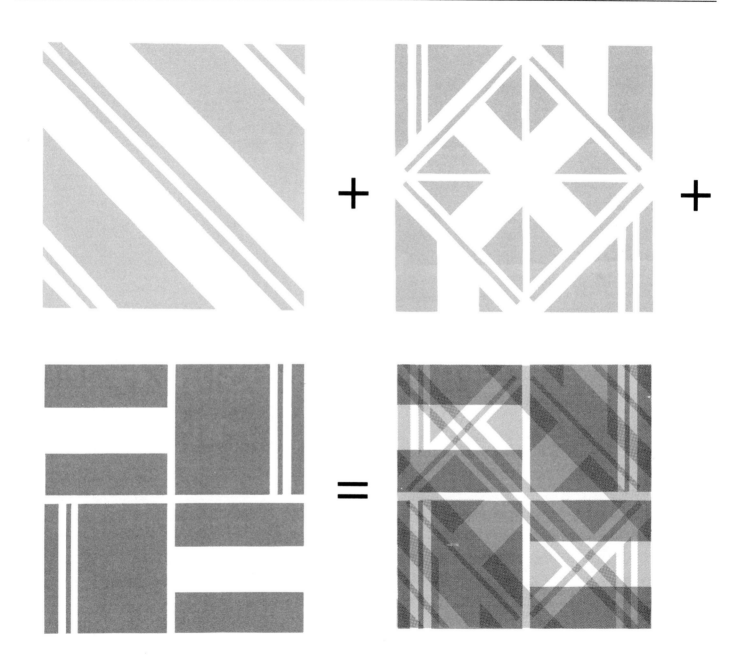

Other Possibilities

☞ Change a black-and-white portrait—or any piece of art—into a color one. Make two or more copies in black, then white out different parts of each copy and have them printed in different colors onto a single copy, as explained above. The colors will show up best with a fairly dense scene—one without a lot of open space.

☞ Make the double portrait described at the beginning of this chapter using two different colors.

☞ Superimpose words or quotations in more than one color.

☞ Create an abstract composition in several colors. For each color, you'll need an original in black and white. One might feature an interesting texture (a bamboo placemat, a wall rubbing). Another might have a single solid shape. A third might have squiggly lines you've drawn. Experiment with different combinations. Have them printed as described above.

CHAPTER • 7

Iron-Ons

T-shirts are to your body what decals are to your car. And just as you can make your own decals, so too can you use the copier to decorate your shirts, make badges, and transfer any artwork you've created to fabric. To do this, you need to have your original copied onto a heat transfer.

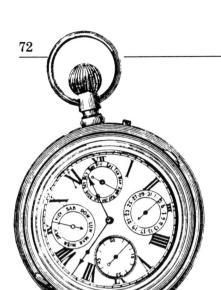

About Heat Transfers

A heat transfer is a specially prepared sheet that will emerge from a color copier with a reversed image of your artwork. You then iron it onto fabric, peel off the backing, and find your right-side-up image on the material.

The most difficult part of using heat transfers might be finding a copy shop that offers them. If your usual shop doesn't, the clerk may know of one that does. You might find that a shop specializing in silk-screening T-shirts can make transfers for you. Open the phone book and call around.

Transfers cost several dollars. At a silk-screening shop, the price given might sound astronomical because it includes a T-shirt. Find out if they'll sell you a transfer alone. Because they require the use of a full-color copier, transfers cost the same amount whether your art is printed in black and white or full color. If you get a dozen beautiful badges from each one, the price will seem a bargain.

The art you choose will be determined by what you plan to iron it onto. For a T-shirt, consider the possibilities listed for decals: parody sights and celebrations, personal statements, etc. Or you might use a design from a clip art book. Whatever you choose, you'll probably want it to fill up most of the sheet so that your art won't be lost on the shirt.

You might decide instead to make a sheet of badges, of the sort Boy Scouts and Girl Scouts have sewn to their uniforms. These can be any shape or size. Like merit badges, they might celebrate the accomplishment of a deed or skill, real or ludicrous. They might testify to your having visited a particular place. Or they might simply bear drawings of something you'd like to add to your clothes: animals, words, designs from heraldry, etc.

For either T-shirts or badges, you could use one of your decals, silhouettes, or other artwork from previous projects.

Step 1.
Plan Your Original

Transfers usually are 8½ x 11 inches or a bit smaller. Check with the shop you're using and lay out your original accordingly. If 8½ x 11 inches isn't large enough for what you have in mind, you could always spread your design over two transfers. This would, however, cost twice as much; it might also prove difficult to iron them on in perfect alignment.

Step 2.
Copy and Paste Up

Copy the art you've chosen, altering it as needed. If you're using words on a T-shirt, use heavy type and enlarge the letters so

Step 2

that they'll be readable. Consider using a border, especially on badges.

Cut out your art and glue it to a sheet of copy paper. Since you'll be using a full-color machine, any guidelines you make should be erased or whited out once you no longer need them. Arrange the badges so you get as many as possible on a page, leaving ¾ inch or so between them on all sides, room you'll need when cutting them out.

Step 3.
Add Color

Full color won't cost extra in this case and will add a lot to your shirt's or badges' looks. When you've finished your pasteup, make several copies of your original. Use these for experimenting with different felt pens until you get the combination of colors you want. You can color around or over words and art if you avoid dark colors. Pastel highlighting pens work well for this.

Make up a final, colored original. You might decide to use one of your multicolor copies from the previous chapter as your final original.

Step 4.
Have the Transfer Made

Take your original to a shop and have the transfer made. Your artwork will appear in reverse. It may be that it will have been reduced slightly to fit onto the transfer. Before you leave, be sure to ask for written instruc-

tions for ironing on the transfer. Most shops that make transfers have these.

Step 5.
Get a T-Shirt or Fabric

For T-shirts, cotton or cotton-polyester fabric in white or light colors works best.

For badges, you'll want heavier fabric. Go to a fabric store and look at the heaviest muslin and the lightest-weight canvas. Interfacing, which is used to stiffen clothing, makes excellent

TRANSFER

badges as well. Again, use only light colors, and avoid fabric with a very rough woven surface. You won't need much—probably no more than an eighth of a yard, which won't cost much at all. You might try a little of several kinds of fabric.

Step 6.

Iron On the Transfer

You'll probably want some adult help with this step. Follow the ironing instructions you were given. If the shop didn't have any, the main points to remember are:

● Because you'll be pressing quite hard, do the ironing on a table or counter, not on an ironing board.

● Put a folded pillowcase on your surface, iron out the wrinkles, then place the fabric you'll be ironing onto on top.

● Cut out the part of the transfer you want to use and place it with the image down on your fabric. With badges, you might want to cut the transfer in two, ironing half the badges onto one kind of fabric and the other half onto another.

● Heat the iron on a fairly high setting. Press it down hard with both hands for ten seconds or so in each of the positions shown, overlapping so as to cover the whole transfer. Do not use steam. If the part of the transfer you're using is small, fewer positions with the iron will be needed.

● After you've covered the whole transfer, reheat it by guiding the iron around the entire surface several times.

● While the transfer is hot, grasp one of the corners and peel the backing away from the fabric, revealing your right-side-up design.

Step 7.

Cut and Sew

If you ironed onto a T-shirt, you're finished. If you made badges, cut them out carefully with scissors, leaving a little room around each edge. Then have an adult help you hem them, if necessary, and sew them onto jackets, sweatshirts, hats, backpacks, or what you will.

To preserve your artwork, don't use bleach on the clothing you affixed it to or iron it after washing. Turning the clothing inside out when washing, and avoiding high washing and drying temperatures, will also help.

Other Possibilities

☞ Iron designs, scenes, or names onto napkins.

☞ Add some appropriate artwork to an apron or pillowcase.

☞ Design and produce your own flags.

CHAPTER • 8

Stamps

Postage stamps are miniature worlds. You might already collect them. With the copier's help, you can create them as well. To copy real United States stamps would, of course, be illegal. But you're free to invent your own country or countries and to add their stamps to your letters. In your hands, the tiny space on a stamp can become a vast and detailed domain.

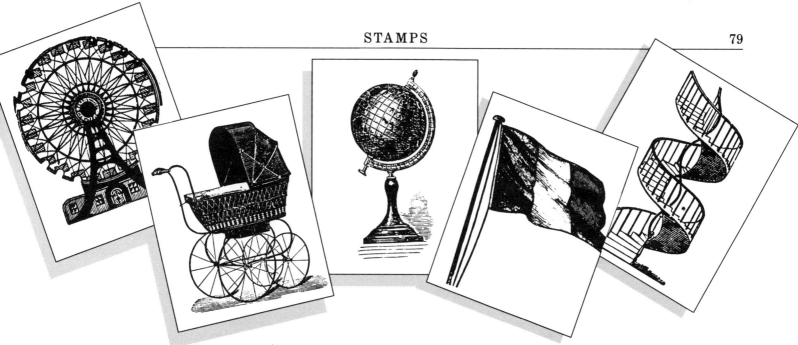

Step 1.

Copy Your Artwork

Your stamps might carry the name of an imaginary country, celebrating its heroes, animals, holidays, or famous sights. Or you could use them to feature the faces of family members, abstract designs, political statements—anything you like. Look at actual stamps to get ideas. Have a look as well at the information on mail art in the books listed in *Recommended Books*. Many copy artists produce their own stamps.

Once you know your subject matter, find the artwork you'll need. Art that must be reduced a great deal will come out much sharper if reduced behind the counter at a copy shop.

To make your stamps look realistic, you'll probably want to use words and numbers: the Latin name of the starfish you're picturing, the stamp's value, etc. Transfer type works well for the number. You might want to make several copies of the complete sheet before you begin, cutting and gluing down the numbers if you run out of transfer figures.

A typewriter or computer will easily produce any words you need. Try spacing out letters, using capitals and lower case, and printing your words in different typefaces. Make several different reductions and enlargements of the words and numbers you want. This will give you many sizes to choose from when you're ready for pasting up.

Step 2.

Pasteup

Your stamps can be any size and any shape that's composed of straight lines. Look at actual stamps to get ideas for arranging what will go on the stamp. Your words might appear upright along one edge, at the top and bottom, or around the entire border. Your numbers might be superimposed on the art, easily accomplished with transfer type. Cut out your artwork and words and paste up your stamp.

If you want to produce a full sheet of identical stamps, use a yellow pen to divide an 8½" x 11" sheet so as to contain as many of the stamps as possible. Remember to leave a little space along the paper's edge. This sheet will be your final original. Next, go to a copy shop. If you can get forty stamps on a page, for example, you would make forty copies, cut them all out, and glue them down. To save time and money, you might simply have five copies made, paste them up, filling one row of your final original, and then have eight copies of this made, pasting up the other rows in place. Some shops have a laser machine that can take a single row of stamps you've pasted up

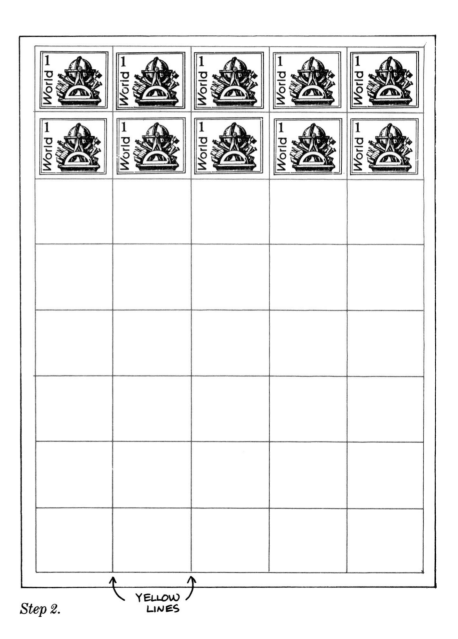

Step 2.

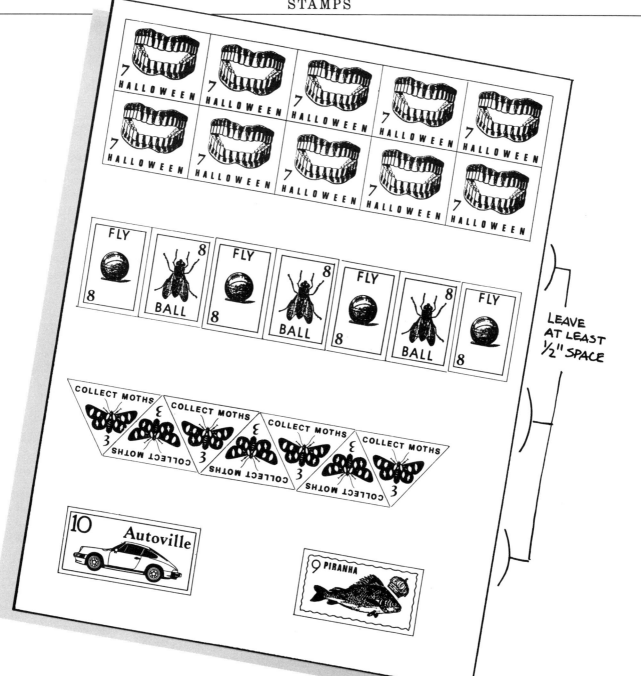

LEAVE AT LEAST ½" SPACE

and produce a full page of stamps—a stamp maker's dream. Call around and check the price first.

If you want several different stamps instead of a sheet of identical stamps, use a yellow pen to lay them out on a sheet of copy paper. To make perforating the stamps easier in Step 5, leave ½ inch between stamps of different shapes and avoid an arrangement resembling a brick wall. Glue down your artwork within the yellow lines. You might decide to make five copies of a stamp you like, ten copies of one you like even more, and one apiece of several others.

Step 3.
Copy Your Stamps

Take your final original to a copy shop and have it copied. Consider using colored paper, or having it printed in a color rather than black, or both. If you have it copied onto a white 8½" x 11" adhesive sheet, you could then simply peel off the backing and stick the stamps to envelopes rather than glue them. Unfortunately, it's often difficult to remove small cutouts from the backing sheet.

Step 4.
Perforate Your Stamps

The rows of holes dividing stamps are called perforations. You can easily perforate your own stamps and so make them look quite real. All you need is an inexpensive tool called a tracing wheel, sold at fabric shops and other stores with sewing supplies. Get the kind with tiny metal teeth.

Place a folded newspaper on a table or desk, put your sheet of stamps on top, and with a ruler to guide you, move the tracing wheel back and forth several times between the stamps, pressing firmly. Try not to let the

Step 4.

ruler move. If you start the tracing wheel at slightly different points, your perforations will be much closer together, which in turn will make it easier to remove the stamps from the sheet.

Your stamps are now ready to use. Glue them to your envelopes. Send them as gifts. Trade them with other copy artists. Just don't forget to put a *real* stamp on your letters!

Other Possibilities

☞ To make full-color stamps, add color to your final original with felt pens, then have it copied on a full-color machine.

☞ Paste up a scene that extends over several stamps. You might even use a single piece of art, enlarged or reduced to 8½ x 11 inches, as your original. Have it copied onto a label or paper, then perforate it into stamps of whatever shape and size you wish.

☞ Using rubber stamps, for words or images or both, can save a lot of copying and pasting up, especially if you're making many stamps. You'll have to adapt the postage stamp's size to your rubber stamp. If the impression isn't perfect, you can add lines with a pen. However, you won't be able to move the rubber stamp's impression if it's out of place, as you can when pasting up copied art.

CHAPTER 9

Flip Books

F

lip books are hand-held movies. By viewing the slightly different scenes on the pages you flip, you seem to behold a moving subject. To make your own, you need many identical images of a subject—difficult and time-consuming to draw, but a snap to produce with a copier.

About Flip Books

When planning your flip book, keep in mind that the action you'll be showing must be very gradual. The less change between one card and the next, the more realistic the action will seem. Because only part of each card is seen, the scene must also be fairly small. The nearer you keep the action to the right-hand edge, the more easily seen it will be. Try to choose a scene whose motion can be easily shown and whose artwork you think you can find. Sometimes it will be easier to draw in some part of a scene by hand than to find it in a book: a line representing a road, a hole in a rink into which a skater disappears, etc.

Many types of scenes lend themselves to flip books. This chapter will show you how to make two different kinds, then give you some ideas for others. Before you begin, make the following layout sheet.

Make Your Layout Sheet

With a ruler and a black pen, divide an 8½" x 11" sheet of copy paper as shown. Each compartment will be one card. Think of them as numbered from one to twelve. Because one sheet won't give you enough cards to show very much action, you'll need two sheets to make a flip book—twenty-three cards, plus a title card. For a longer flip book, use three or more sheets.

Make as many copies of this layout sheet as you think you'll need.

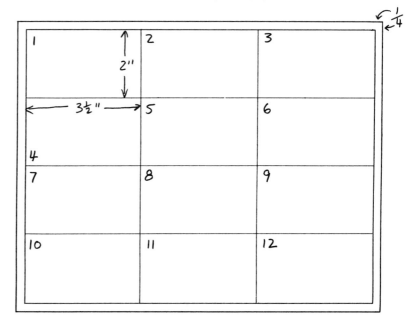

Layout sheet

Flip Book #1

This flip book will show an airplane making a loop in the air. It requires only one piece of art copied many times. This is the easiest type of flip book to make.

Step 1.
Find Artwork

All you need is a drawing of an airplane seen from the side. If you can't find one in a clip art book, use your library's card catalog to find books about airplanes.

Step 2.
Make Copies

Reduce the plane to one inch or less in length. You'll then need twenty-four copies. To save money, you could make four copies, cut them out, glue them onto one page, and then make six copies of this sheet.

Step 3.
Paste Up Your Title Card

You'll use two layout sheets for this flip book. Card number one on the first sheet will be your title card. Choose a title you like. You could write the words or glue down typed words. You might want to include the drawing of the plane. Consider a border or ornament as well.

Step 4.
Divide Up the Action

You have twenty-three cards in which to show the airplane approaching from the left, making a loop, and flying off the page

toward the right. Your scene will be half over when you reach the first card on the second sheet. With a yellow pen, make a mark on the left-hand side of that card. Your plane should be upside down, in the middle of its loop, at

that point. Make a mark on the sixth card before and the sixth card after this card; these are the cards on which you'll begin and end the loop. This will leave you five cards apiece to show the plane approaching and leaving.

Step 5.
Draw Guidelines

Positioning your art carefully will make the scene look realistic. A ruler and yellow pen make this

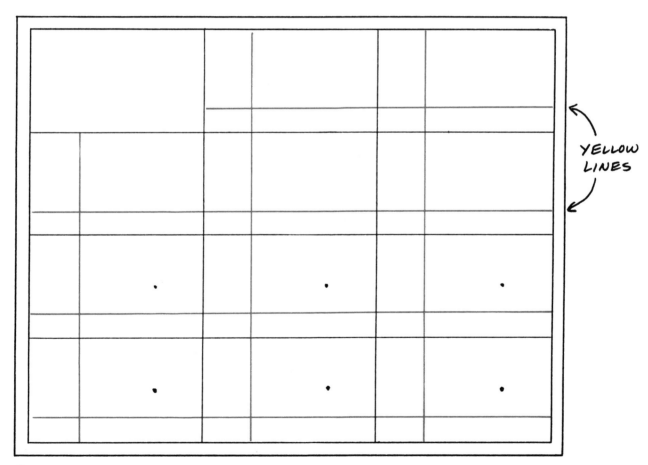

YELLOW
LINES

Step 5

easy to do. First, draw a vertical line 1 inch to the right of each card's left side. To be seen, all your artwork must be placed to the right of these lines. Next, draw a horizontal line ½ inch from the bottom of each card. This will help you keep the plane straight. On the card in which the plane begins its loop, make a dot with the yellow pen where you imagine the center of the loop to be. This should be roughly 1 inch from the card's top and right sides. Then make dots in the same place on the other loop cards.

Step 6.
Paste Up the Scene

You're now ready to make your movie. Cut out all the airplanes, then begin gluing them down as shown on pages 90 and 91. Your first plane should be just crossing the vertical yellow line, so that only its front will be seen. The second plane should be about ¼ inch or so to the right of the

first, and so on. Use the horizontal guidelines to keep them flying straight. Space out the loop in similar fashion, keeping the plane flying around the yellow dots. It should be upside down on the second sheet's first card. After the loop, have it resume its straight flight and gradually disappear beyond the right edge. Your last card might show just its tail, or nothing at all.

Once you've finished, look over the sheets and do any last-minute whiting out or adding.

Step 7.
Copy Your Originals

Take your two sheets to a copy shop and have a copy (or more) of each sheet made onto card stock. Card stock comes in various weights. Ask for the lightest weight available, which will give you cards that flip easily.

Step 8.
Cut Out the Cards

With your knife or a paper cutter, cut the card stock along the black lines. The ¼ inch strips along the sides won't be part of the flip book. Try to keep the cards in order as you cut and stack them. By making your vertical cuts a hair to the left of the black lines, you'll keep those lines from showing on the right side of your movie.

Step 6.

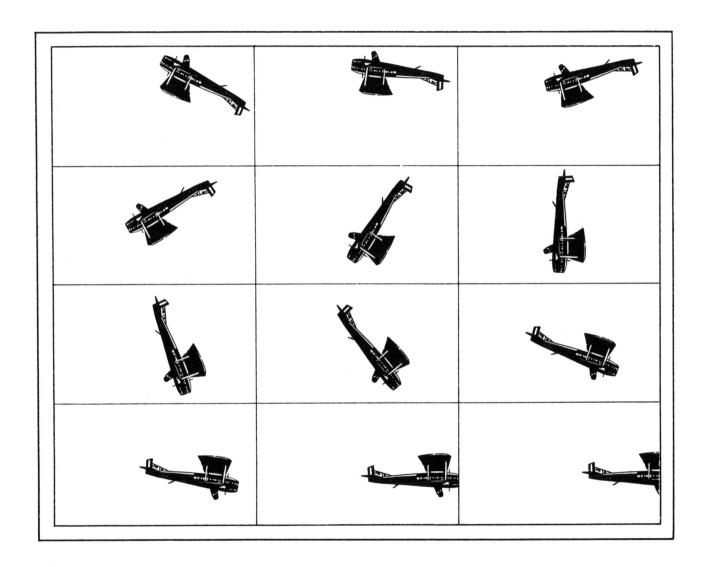

Step 9.
Assemble the Cards

Put the cards in order, with the title card on top. Jiggle the cards on a table to get the cards' right sides even. Slip a rubber band over the left side of the cards. Hold the stack with your left hand, run your right thumb down the right-hand side—and behold your airplane making its midair loop.

For a small charge, a copy shop will staple your stack, so you won't lose any cards. You could also have them trim the stack, leaving all the sides perfectly even.

Other Possibilities

☞ A hummingbird making a figure eight

☞ A hot-air balloon traveling up and out of sight

☞ A bird chasing and catching a flying insect (which then disappears)

☞ Consider adding an unmoving prop or bit of scenery. This would allow you to picture a figure jumping on a trampoline, frogs hopping from one lily pad to another, a man being fired out of a cannon, etc.

☞ Try making two copies on card stock of each original. This won't add any new action, but will make the action you have seem smoother, since your eye will more likely glimpse every card.

☞ If you can find a rubber stamp of the subject you want, you can stamp the figure in black ink on each card. This will save you making copies of the figure and pasting them up.

Flip Book #2

This type of flip book will give you an extremely realistic view of a man doing a somersault, a dog running at full speed, or a similar figure in motion. In the previous flip book, you created the motion by positioning identical figures in different places on the cards. With this flip book, you'll paste up a sequence of different scenes in the same place on the cards.

Step 1.
Find Artwork

You'll need to find a sequence of drawings or photographs of a figure in motion. These can usually be found in a library. Look for a book (or article) about Eadweard Muybridge, a man who specialized in photographing people and animals in motion. You might find a book of his photographic sequences, or a book about him among the biographies. Check as well in books on the history of photography, the history of motion pictures, and in books about old-fashioned toys, some of which made use of such scenes of motion. Looking up "Muybridge" or "zoetrope" (one such toy) in the index of such a book may lead you to what you're after. Checking the bibliography for other books on the subject might do the same. Remember to look in both the children's and adult sections. An encyclopedia article might show one of the sequences as well.

Choose a scene in which the figure is in profile. Look for one with a white background, or a background with so few details that you could white them out without too much trouble. Look also for a sequence that can be

On Your Mark
Get Set....
GO!

YELLOW
LINES

Step 5.

repeated indefinitely: a horse galloping, a windmill turning, or a dog running, as shown in the layout on page 94. A man throwing a javelin can't be repeated (unless he's shown going to get it and picking it up) and would make for too short a flip book.

Step 2.
Copy Your Artwork

You'll paste up your art on two layout sheets. Reduce or enlarge your sequence to fit onto the right portion of the cards. Then white out any background details and make several copies of the entire sequence—enough to give you a total of at least twenty-three individual images. If you want your flip book to be longer, make more copies.

Step 3.
Paste Up Your Title Card

See Step 3 for Flip Book 1.

Step 4.
Draw Guidelines

You'll position all your images in about the same spot, close to the cards' right edges. Draw horizontal guidelines with a yellow pen through all the cards. This will help keep your figure's motion looking smooth.

Step 5.
Paste Up the Scene

Number the individual images with a yellow pen. Then cut them out and paste them up in order, using the guidelines to help you position them. After you've finished, check your two final originals for any needed whiting out or adding.

Step 6.
Copy, Cut, and Assemble

See Steps 7, 8, and 9 for Flip Book 1.

Another Possibility

☞ Combine two moving figures (a bull charging left to right and a bird flying above him right to left, etc.)

Other Types of Flip Books

Try some of these other ideas, using what you've learned making the first two flip books.

Moving figure and stationary background

This is like Flip Book 1, except that the figure is superimposed against a background. If you want to show a skier coming down a mountain, for example, make twenty-three copies of the mountain scene and paste them up in the same place on the cards. Next, find a skier, enlarge or reduce, and fill in the figure with a black pen, making it a silhouette.

Paste up a sheet with twenty-three copies of the skier and have a transparency made of this. Cut out the skiers. Using Scotch Magic tape (dull, not shiny), tape them over the mountain scene, advancing the skier slightly on each card. Making the skier a silhouette will keep the background scene from being seen through his or her body. If you have a rubber stamp of your figure, you could use that and then fill in each figure with a pen.

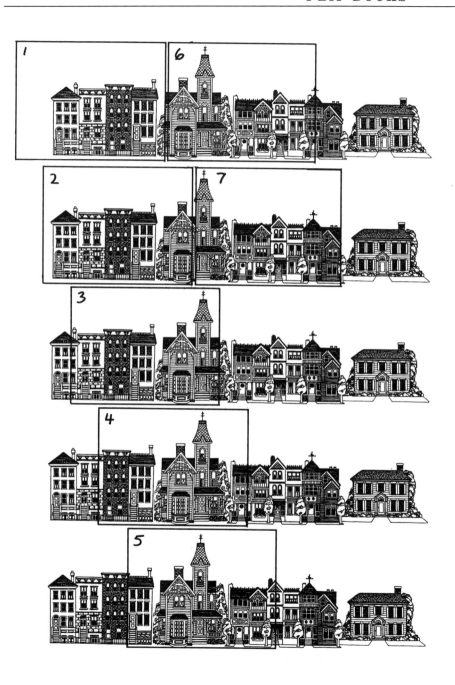

Stationary figure and moving background

This style of flip book requires a figure who travels only in a straight line (unlike the skier above), but lets your figure take a much longer journey, through a variety of backgrounds if you wish. Make five copies of a long background scene: a city street, country landscape, ocean scene, etc. Then use a piece of transparency cut to 2 x 2½ inches to trace around parts of the scenes in sequence with a yellow pen, moving the transparency ahead ½ inch each time. You'll need to switch from copy to copy. Number each scene after tracing around it. Cut these out and glue them down in order. Then choose a figure to pass through this scene: a taxi, boat, bicyclist, walker. As above, reduce or enlarge, fill in with black, and make a transparency with twenty-three copies of the figure. Cut out the figures and tape them over the background scenes, keeping the figure in the same place on each card—which means in a different part of the background. If you have a rubber stamp of the figure, use that instead and then fill in each one with a pen. When you flip the cards, the moving background will trick your eye into thinking the figure is moving.

Approaching and receding figures

By making many different reductions or enlargements of a figure seen from the front, then pasting them up in order of size, beginning with the smallest, you can make the figure seem to be

coming closer and closer. By doing the reverse with a figure seen from the back, you can make the figure seem to be departing into the distance. Consider having both types of motion on each card, or figures traveling at different speeds, or figures whose open mouths devour the viewer on the final card.

An artist at work

Make twenty-three copies of a reduction of a famous painting, and twenty-three copies of a hand holding a paintbrush. Use correction tape and whiteout to hide all, then

most, then less and less of the painting. By positioning the brush at the whiteout's edge, you can create the illusion that the hand is painting the masterpiece that's gradually revealed.

Words

Make a flip book that shows a message unfolding. The words might move in a line from right to left, or in curves or spirals. Design a message, make several copies, then follow the technique used with the stationary figure and moving background flip book above, without adding a stationary figure.

CHAPTER 10

Films

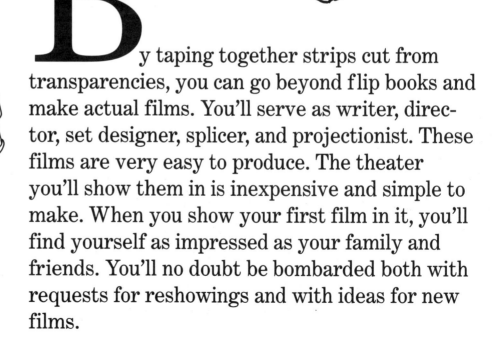

By taping together strips cut from transparencies, you can go beyond flip books and make actual films. You'll serve as writer, director, set designer, splicer, and projectionist. These films are very easy to produce. The theater you'll show them in is inexpensive and simple to make. When you show your first film in it, you'll find yourself as impressed as your family and friends. You'll no doubt be bombarded both with requests for reshowings and with ideas for new films.

Building the Theater

You'll probably need to make a trip to a hardware or lumber store for the theater's parts. You might need a bit of adult help as well. You'll need:

Supplies

- 2 pieces of wood, 8½" x 11" x ¾"
- 2 pieces of wood, 8½" x ¾" x ¾"

- 6 bolts, ¼" x 2½"
- 2 metal washers for ¼" bolts

- 4 rubber bumpers, at least ¼" high, with screws to fit
- 4 pushpins
- 2 spools
- 4 nails, at least 1" long
- Sandpaper
- Drill and ¼" bit
- Screwdriver
- Hammer

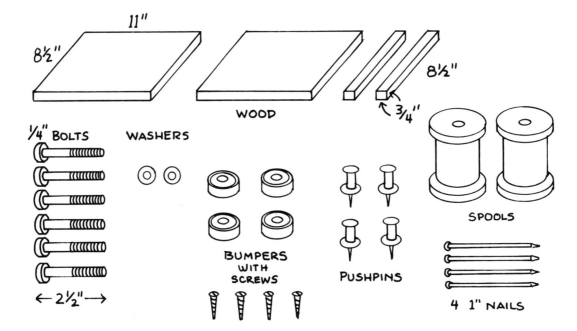

11"

8½"

WOOD

8½"

¾"

¼" BOLTS   WASHERS

BUMPERS
WITH
SCREWS

PUSHPINS

SPOOLS

← 2½" →

4 1" NAILS

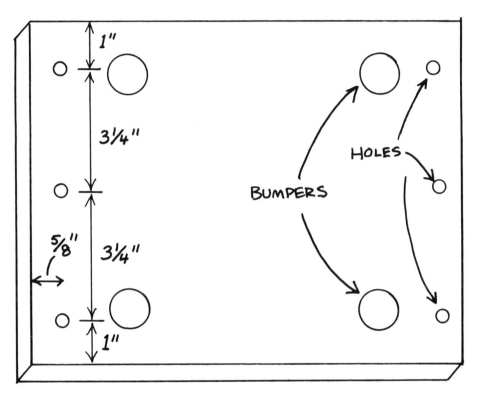

VIEW OF BOTTOM OF BASE

The large pieces of wood could be thinner or thicker than ¾ inch. The thin pieces of wood can also be larger or smaller than ¾ x ¾ inch. It doesn't matter how much threading is on the bolts.

Step 1.
Sand and Drill

Sand all sides of the pieces of wood. One of the large pieces will be the theater's base. The base's upper side should be flat and smooth so that your films won't

catch on anything. Drill six ¼-inch holes through this piece as shown. Sand any rough places around the holes.

Step 2.
Attach Bumpers

Screw in the rubber bumpers on the underside where they won't be in the way of the holes, and where their screws won't collide with the nails you'll use to attach the posts. The base will sit on the bumpers rather than on the bolts.

Step 3.
Attach Back and Posts

The other large piece of wood will be the theater's back. Nail it to the back of the base, aligned at the bottom with the base's bottom. The thin pieces of wood will serve as posts for the theater's front, which you'll make later. Nail them to the front of the base at the corners.

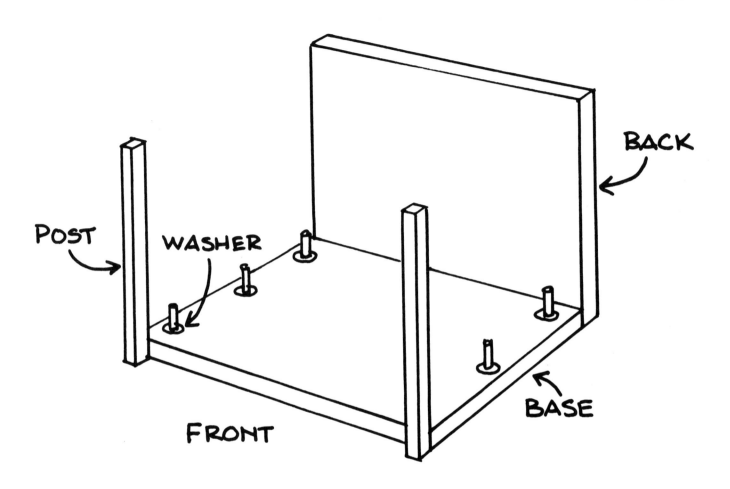

Step 4.

Insert Bolts

Next, push the bolts up through the holes. It may be a tight squeeze. Tap them through with a hammer if you need to, but don't use a file to enlarge the holes, since you want the bolts to fit snugly enough to stay in place. Slip the washers over any two of the bolts for the moment. Your theater is finished. If you wish, you can paint the base and back white, which will make the images on your films easier to see.

Making a Film

This sample film will show ice skaters in action. After the instructions, you'll find a list of other possible subjects and types of films—a list to which you can add your own discoveries.

Step 1.

Lay Out Your Original

With a yellow pen, draw guide-lines on a sheet of 8½" x 11" copy paper as shown. Then take a black pen and draw over a tiny

Step 1.

bit of each yellow line close to the paper's edge on either side. These black marks will guide you when you cut out your film.

Step 2.
Find Your Artwork

For this film you'll need every drawing of ice skaters that you can find. There are clip art books devoted entirely to sporting scenes. Try as well the clip art collections listed in *Recommended Books*. At the library, look through books on skating, the history of sports, and any books (fiction or nonfiction) that might show winter scenes. Try to find seven or eight different skaters. Silhouettes are fine. It doesn't matter if the skaters are facing in different directions or seen from different angles.

Step 3.
Copy Your Artwork

You'll need to reduce or enlarge your skaters until they're slightly shorter than one inch. If some of your skaters are much larger than this, have the reducing done behind the counter at a copy shop so that you won't lose too much detail.

Once all the skaters are the right size, paste them up all on one sheet and make four copies of it.

Step 4.
Paste Up Your Film

You've laid out eight horizontal strips on your original, each 1 inch wide. You won't use the ¼-inch strips at the top and bottom of the page. You'll glue your skaters onto the strips, have transparencies made, cut the strips out, then tape them together to make your film.

Let's suppose you want to show just a single skater on the ice, then another, then many more, then the crowd thinning out until your first skater again skates alone and departs. To do this, paste up only the first skater on your original's first strip. Since you'll be cutting along the yellow lines, make certain the figure's feet and head aren't touching these. On the second strip, paste up two widely spaced skaters. Don't place any figures so close to the edge that they're beyond the small black marks you made.

On the third, fourth, and fifth strips you can add more and more skaters. You'll soon need to repeat certain skaters. It doesn't matter which way they're facing, since skaters can skate backward as well as forward. Paste up fewer skaters on the sixth and seventh strip, and only your first skater on the last strip.

Your film is nearly finished.

Step 4.

Look it over and do any whiting out or adding that's called for.

Step 5.

Make Transparencies

Go to a copy shop and have a transparency made of your original. For a longer film make two transparencies. Buy a blank transparency as well. Try to keep all of these clean and free of fingerprints.

Step 6.

Cut the Transparencies

With your knife or a paper cutter, cut your transparencies into strips, using the black marks you made as guides. Cut the blank transparency into 1 x 11-inch strips as well. Then make vertical cuts to snip the black guide marks off the strips.

Step 7.

Tape the Strips

Take your strips to a clean workplace. Tape two of the blank strips together as shown, without overlapping them. If the strips are not all exactly one inch wide, keep the bottoms of the strips even, letting any discrepancies appear at the top. This will allow your film to roll smoothly. Shiny Scotch tape matches the plastic of transparencies better than other types. Bending the tape under the strips, then pressing it firmly on the other side, will also make for a

smooth screening.

Tape two more blank strips to the film's right end. Your film will begin to grow in length. Put down a clean towel or something similar for it to lie on once it slides off the table and reaches the floor.

After the four blank strips, add the strips with the skaters. You could use the strips from just one of your transparencies, taped together in order. Or you could make a longer film, with more crowd scenes, by adding strips three through six from the second transparency to the middle of your film. These could be flipped over left to right so that

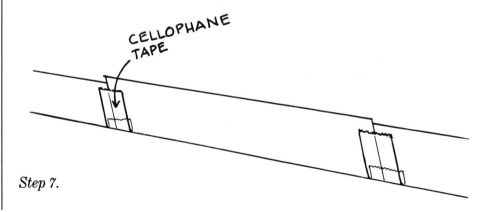

CELLOPHANE TAPE

Step 7.

their skaters are heading in the opposite direction of their mates from the first transparency.

After you've reached your final skater, attach the other four blank strips. Your film is finished. Wind it up and put a rubber band around it to hold it while you see to the last two things you'll need.

Step 8.

Wind Film onto Spools

You'll need two empty spools to wind your film onto. These can be wooden or plastic. Try to find a large size. Those that are 1⅝ inches high and 1½ inches in diameter are perfect. If you don't have any around the house, you can always buy two spools of thread and wind the thread onto something else.

The spools will serve as your film's reels. A pushpin pressed down into the top of each of them, near the edge, makes a good handle. Nearly all spools

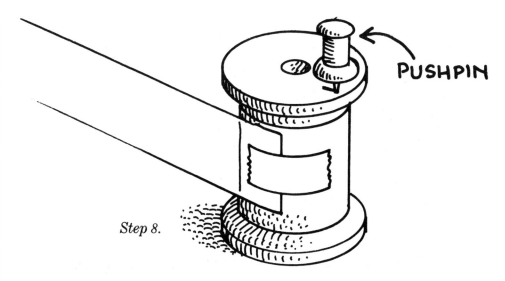

Step 8.

have a ¼-inch hole in the center and will fit over the theater's bolts. You may have to remove a label to reveal the hole.

Remove the rubber band from your film. Tape the end of the film to one of the spools. Then wind the film onto the spool and put the rubber band back over it.

Step 9.

Make the Theater's Front

A real movie theater has a curtain. Yours will have a piece of card stock into which you've cut an opening for viewing.

Take a sheet of 8½" x 11" copy paper and with a black pen draw the lines shown on page 108. You'll cut along these lines later. Next, paste up whatever words and ornaments you want to appear. You could make a separate front for each film, featuring the film's title and perhaps a figure who appears in it. Or you could make a front that serves for all films, giving the name of the theater, the price of tickets, and such. A border around the opening sets it off nicely.

PUSHPIN

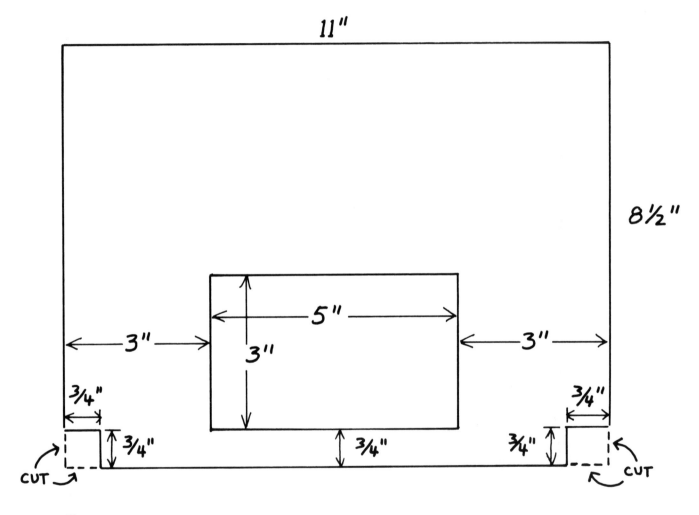

Step 9.

ICE PALACE

Clip art theater front.

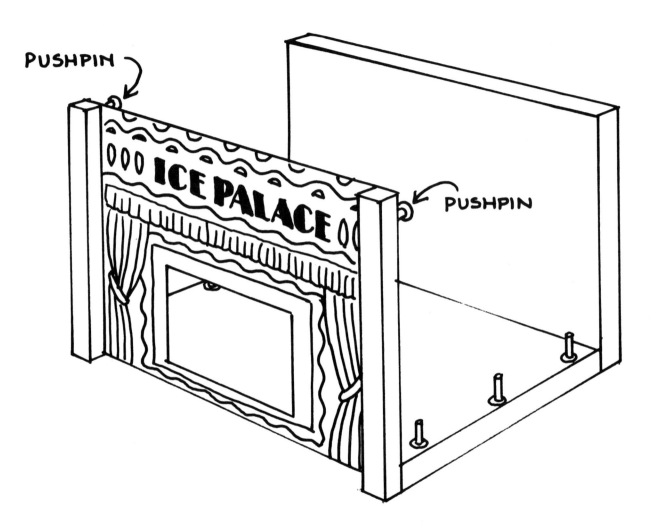

PUSHPIN

PUSHPIN

Once you've finished pasting up, have your original copied onto card stock. Then use your ruler and knife to cut out the opening and the corner pieces, cutting away the black lines so that they don't show on the front. Slip the front behind the posts, attaching it to them with push-pins. The bottom of the opening should be even with or just above the top of the theater's base.

Showtime!

At last you're ready to show your film. This type of film, as you'll see, can be shown in several different ways.

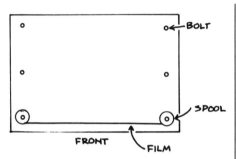

Method #1

Put the washers on the two front bolts. Take the rubber band off the loaded spool and slip the spool over one of the front bolts. Put the empty spool on the other front bolt, unwind the film a bit, and tape the free end to the empty spool. You'll probably want to arrange the spools so that the film passes from the front of one spool to the front of the other, rather than at an angle. Have your audience look straight into the theater's open-ing. The spools and bolts should be hidden by the front. Turn the empty spool's handle and your figures will come skating across the ice. The threads on the bolts won't hurt your film.

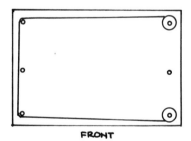

Method #2

At a rink, people usually skate in circles. You can duplicate this motion by placing your spools and winding the film around the bolts as shown. The washers always go under the spools. Because you've used transparen-cies, your audience can look through the front of the film and see the figures in the rear. The sense of depth and multiplied motion is exciting.

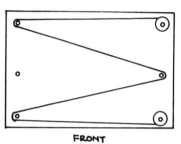

Method #3

Skaters on a pond or lake are of-ten zooming in all directions. By threading your film as shown, your audience will see *four* strips of skaters moving simultane-ously. This method is the most captivating of all and will proba-bly receive the loudest applause. The film you made, with four blank strips at each end, was de-signed for this method. You could, of course, drill more holes and insert more bolts to increase the chaos on the ice. To still have your first skater appear alone at the beginning and end, you'd need to add more blank strips.

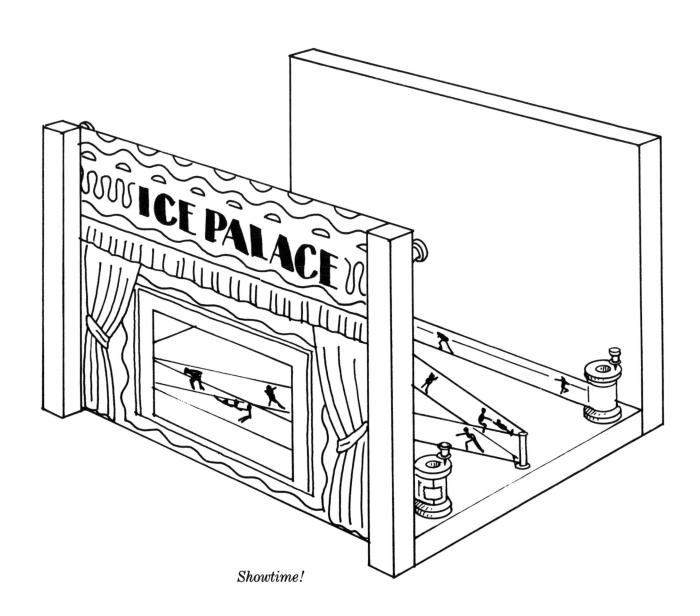

Showtime!

Other Possibilities

☞ If you had no luck in finding ice skaters, try dancers on a dance floor, fish in a tank, or soccer players on a field (keeping only one ball in view at a time).

☞ Use the cars, pedestrians, and animals from the time-exposure scene in Chapter 6 to make a film of a busy street. Use Method #3.

☞ Make a one-minute condensation of a famous ballet or opera.

☞ Have the words of a song pass from right to left, with images of some of the things mentioned in the text appearing above the words. Use Method #1.

☞ Make a theater front that resembles the inside of a train compartment, with two window openings. Use Method #1 to show the sights seen out the window during the journey. You could design a trip that goes from the east coast to the west, across Europe, or wherever you like.

☞ Movies have soundtracks; yours can have one too. Find a recording of the "Blue Danube" waltz to play while you show your skating film. During your one-minute ballet you could play the ballet's music at high speed. Libraries often have recordings of the ocean, city streets, and other sound effects.

☞ Record your own words on a soundtrack and make a filmstrip, complete with chimes (or the sound of your choice) signaling when to advance the film to the next picture. A lecture on the process of digestion, with artwork from a medical book? An account of a journey? An illustrated story you've written? Use Method #1.

CHAPTER 11

More Ideas

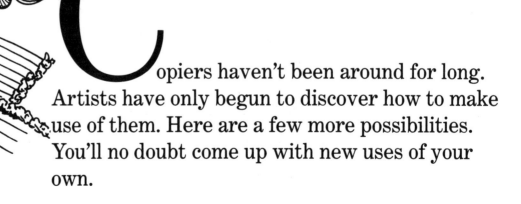

Copiers haven't been around for long. Artists have only begun to discover how to make use of them. Here are a few more possibilities. You'll no doubt come up with new uses of your own.

Stencils

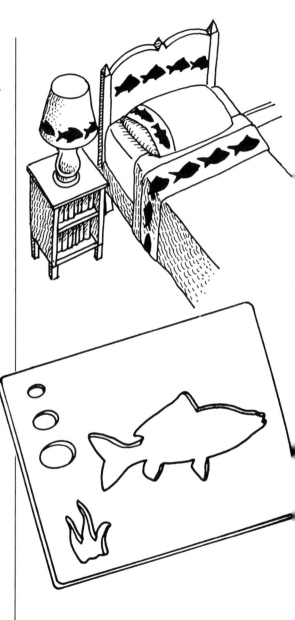

Stenciling is an easy way to decorate paper, fabric, furniture, and walls. Traditionally, stencil designs are cut out of heavy paper. The stencil is then laid on a surface and paint applied in the cutout area. This allows a shape to be reproduced many times.

You can buy books of ready-to-use stencils. But even heavy paper gets bent and torn. You might also never find a book with the particular subject you want or a subject in the size you want. The answer to these problems is the transparency. It's plastic and much more durable than paper. By copying onto it, you can make a stencil of any subject you can find in a book—reduced or enlarged to just the size you want.

First, find the piece of artwork you want. Since it's only the outline you're concerned with, the sharpness of the art, the background, and other details aren't important. Reduce or enlarge as you desire, then have the art copied onto a transparency. With your knife, carefully cut around the edge of the subject, remove it, and you're ready to stencil. If your stencil subjects aren't too large, you'll be able to get more than one on each transparency. By flipping the stencil over, you can make your subject face in the opposite direction.

Collages

Collages are the casseroles of art, mixtures of many different textures and materials. Copiers can assist in several ways.

They can give you copies of artwork you want to include, essential when the art appears in books (which you won't want to take your knife to). Copiers can also supply you with images of textures. Experiment with copying woven placemats, napkins, wood, screening, leaves, and other objects, making certain not to use anything that might scratch the machine's glass. Experiment with color and transparencies.

The parts of a collage are usually glued in place, often overlapping. Consider letting the copier join the parts for you by copying them together. Without gluing, arrange them on the glass, overlapping the pieces as you think best. Make a copy, move things around, enlarge or reduce, and perhaps make another copy. Adding transparencies will increase the sum of images. You can see many imaginative collages in the books listed under "Professional Copy Artists" on page 121.

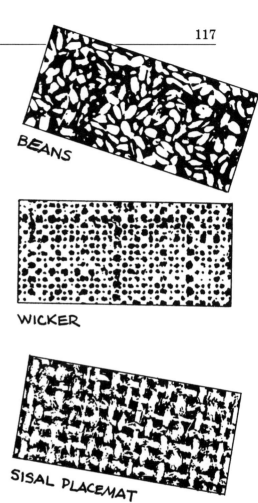

BEANS

WICKER

SISAL PLACEMAT

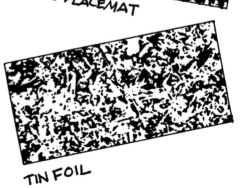

TIN FOIL

Mobiles

Shapes cut out of transparencies make wonderful mobiles, especially if you've copied artwork onto them in color. Use a hole punch to make holes for attaching thread or wire. Hanging in a sunny window, they'll glow like stained glass. You can also use artwork copied onto card stock or glued onto cardboard, foam-core board, or heavier materials.

Bumper Stickers

You can add to your car's artwork by making your own bumper stickers. Have your original copied onto an 8½" x 11" adhesive sheet. This is white, with a peel-off backing, and is inexpensive and available at most copy shops. You can get two 4¼-x-11 inch bumper stickers from each sheet. Your words will need to be large and heavy to be legible.

COPIER CAT

MOGUL MASHER ON BOARD

Recommended Books

Clip Art—General Collections

These books have drawings of many subjects: animals, people, machines, buildings, clothing, etc. Owning one of them can save many trips to the library.

Heck, J. G. *The* *Complete Encyclopedia of Illustration.* New York: Crown/Outlet Book Co., 1979.
This is the best single-volume collection of clip art. Check for it at used-book stores.

Hornung, Clarence. *Handbook of Early Advertising Art*, 3rd rev. ed. New York: Dover Publications, Inc., 1956.
Volume I of this set has drawings; Volume II has old typefaces.

Quinn, Gerard. *The Clip Art Book.* New York: Crown/Crescent Books, 1990.

Clip Art— Particular Subjects

Dover Publications has published many excellent paperback books of clip art, borders, alphabets, and designs. The art is sharp, the books inexpensive. Below are just a few of the dozens available. For a complete catalog, write to

Dover Publications, Inc., 31 East 2nd Street, Mineola, NY 11501.

Grafton, Carol Belanger. *Banners, Ribbons, & Scrolls: An Archive for Designers* (1983).

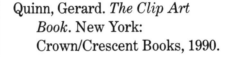

————. *Children: A Pictorial Archive from Nineteenth-Century Sources* (1978).

———. *Old-Fashioned Sports Illustrations* (1988).

———. *Ready-to-Use Small Frames and Borders* (1982).

———. *Silhouettes: A Pictorial Archive of Varied Illustrations* (1979).

Harter, Jim, ed. *Animals: Illustrations of Mammals, Birds, Fish, Insects, Etc.* (1979).

———. *Hands: A Pictorial Archive from Nineteenth-Century Sources* (1985). This book is ideal when you need a drawing of a hand pointing, writing, shaking another hand, etc.

———. *Transportation: A Pictorial Archive from Nineteenth-Century Sources* (1984).

Montgomery Ward & Co. *Catalog and Buyer's Guide No. 57, Spring and Summer 1895* (1969).

This book is a treasure trove of toys, tools, hats, fishing reels, tuning forks, spittoons, and everything in between. Old catalogs from Sears, Roebuck have likewise been reprinted by publishers. Used-book stores often have these.

Professional Copy Artists

Many contemporary artists have made use of copiers. Looking through these books will give you ideas for new copy art projects.

Carstensen, Jeanne. "Mail Art." *Whole Earth Review*, Winter 1987, pp. 84–86. The mail art movement

treats mail as an art form and mobile gallery. By sending out your homemade postcards, stamps, and other creations, you can take part and receive art from all over the world sent by other mail artists. This article and *Correspondence Art* (see below) will tell you all about it.

Firpo, Patrick, Lester Alexander, and Claudia Katayanagi. *Copyart: The First Complete Guide to the Copy Machine.* New York: Richard Marek Publishers, 1978.
This book covers techniques for copy artists and presents a large and exciting selection of copy art, much of it making use of photographs.

Hockney, David. *David Hockney: A Retrospective.* R. B. Kitaj and Henry Geldzahler, eds. New York: Harry N. Abrams, Inc., 1988.
One of the best-known artists of our time, David Hockney became intrigued with the color copier. At the end of this book is a selection of his copy art, produced by the method described for color overlays in Chapter 6.

Stofflet, Mary, and Michael Crane. *Correspondence Art: Source Book for the Network of International Postal Art Activity.* San Francisco: The Contemporary Arts Center, 1984.